Date: 6/4/14

Check out these other networking titles by Andrea Nierenberg!

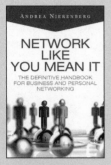

Network Like You Mean It: The Definitive Handbook for Business and Personal Networking

Andrea Nierenberg

ISBN-10:0133742903 | ISBN-13:9780133742909

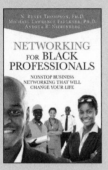

Networking for Black Professionals: Nonstop Business Networking That Will Change Your Life

Michael Lawrence Faulkner
Renee Thompson
Andrea Nierenberg

ISBN-10:013376012X | ISBN-13:9780133760125

Networking for Every College Student and Graduate: Starting Your Career Off Right

Michael Lawrence Faulkner
Andrea Nierenberg

ISBN-10:0133741133 | ISBN-13:9780133741131

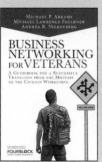

*Business Networking for Veterans:
A Guidebook for a Successful Transition from the Military to the Civilian Workforce*

Michael P. Abrams
Michael Lawrence Faulkner
Andrea Nierenberg

ISBN-10:0133741613 | ISBN-13:9780133741612

ESSENTIAL BUSINESS NETWORKING

ESSENTIAL BUSINESS NETWORKING

Tips, Tactics, and Tools You Can Use

Andrea R. Nierenberg

Vice President, Publisher: Tim Moore
Associate Publisher and Director of Marketing: Amy Neidlinger
Operations Specialist: Jodi Kemper
Cover Designer: Chuti Prasertsith
Development Editor: Russ Hall
Managing Editor: Kristy Hart
Project Editor: Elaine Wiley
Copy Editor: Bart Reed
Proofreader: Sarah Kearns
Indexer: Lisa Stumpf
Compositor: Nonie Ratcliff
Manufacturing Buyer: Dan Uhrig

For information about buying this title in bulk quantities, or for special sales opportunities (which may include electronic versions; custom cover designs; and content particular to your business, training goals, marketing focus, or branding interests), please contact our corporate sales department at corpsales@pearsoned.com or (800) 382-3419.

For government sales inquiries, please contact governmentsales@pearsoned.com.

For questions about sales outside the U.S., please contact international@pearsoned.com.

Company and product names mentioned herein are the trademarks or registered trademarks of their respective owners.

Printed in the United States of America

First Printing January 2014

ISBN-10: 0-13-374288-1
ISBN-13: 978-0-13-374288-6

Pearson Education LTD.
Pearson Education Australia PTY, Limited.
Pearson Education Singapore, Pte. Ltd.
Pearson Education Asia, Ltd.
Pearson Education Canada, Ltd.
Pearson Educación de Mexico, S.A. de C.V.
Pearson Education—Japan
Pearson Education Malaysia, Pte. Ltd.

Library of Congress Control Number: 2013952811

To my wonderful parents, Molly and Paul,
who always taught me life's greatest lessons.

And to all of those who have made strategic networking
a tool for their success in life.

Table of Contents

Acknowledgments

Thank you to Tim Moore, Publisher at Pearson Education, for his hands-on ability to make things happen and for his superior skills that have made many books like this very successful.

A huge thank you to all of the terrific people at Pearson who contributed their amazing skills in pulling this book together. I could never have done this without your help.

Thank you to Russ Hall for his gift in writing and extraordinary editorial talents.

Thank you to Sean Stowers of Pearson Learning Solutions, who thinks out of the box and was the one who "networked" me into the organization and opened the door.

Thank you to Linda Schuler for her excellent administrative and savvy skills.

And a warm and sincere thank you to all the wonderful people in my life who shared their stories and experiences that I incorporated into this book. The list goes on and on—and I thank every single one of you from the bottom of my heart. A special thanks also to two external business partners, who have become very good friends—Annmarie Woods and Al Martella.

Thanks so much to all of you. I am truly blessed.

About the Author

Andrea R. Nierenberg, author, speaker, networking strategist, and business coach and consultant, is the force behind The Nierenberg Consulting Group. Called a "networking success story" by the *Wall Street Journal*, Andrea founded The Nierenberg Consulting Group in 1993.

Her firm provides training in networking, sales, customer service, and presentation skills—all skills that impact the bottom line.

With a stellar 30 years as a leader in sales and marketing, Andrea is an in-demand business expert both at home and abroad. Her firm partners with an array of the world's leading financial and media industry businesses.

Preface

How to Use This Book

Networking is a positive word. Over the years, I have seen many successful people agree that networking is a vital tool for building long-term relationships.

My hope is that *Essential Business Networking* will give you a refresher course and encourage you to implement ways for connecting and reconnecting with people in your life daily, or that it will give you lots of new ideas and suggestions to put into action. There is a wealth of knowledge about the art of networking and relationship marketing in quick sound bites for easy reading and practicing.

This book is a simple read and provides a selection of my top tips organized into chapters representing logical steps for building a powerful network. You don't need to start at the beginning. For example, if you already feel very confident about your business networking skills and want to use this book to meet some new friends, you can leap ahead and start with Chapter 4, "Building Relationships."

Throughout the book, I have added stories from successful friends and colleagues, from whom I have also learned a lot about networking. For example, my good friend and colleague Lois Geller shares this life example:

> "I was on a JetBlue flight and the woman sitting next to me seemed nervous. She was reading from a small book, and I figured she was praying. The ride was turbulent and I asked if she was okay. She told me about her fear of flying, then about her children—she had 11 of them—and soon she forgot about the rough flight. When we left the plane, we exchanged phone numbers and we became friends. Many times when we're together, she tells the story of how I 'saved' her—and she's saved me several times since then."

Was this networking? Absolutely. Sometimes all it takes is just extending an ear, getting into a conversation, anywhere or anytime, to make a connection.

I recommend taking on one tip at a time. Too often when we try to do too much, nothing happens. We get frustrated and don't accomplish anything. Look at the tip that calls out to you and then put it into practice with a true commitment. We live in an ADD (Attention Deficit Disorder) culture, and my hope is that for you, the awareness of true networking becomes almost like oxygen—needed 24/7 with consistency.

Another friend, Daniel, always says, "You don't get it until you do it." He started his networking adventure by "being present" at everything—from industry events to in-house management meetings. As he met people and reached out to them, he realized, "I have to be the one to take the initiative and start the process."

I always say that it takes time to develop and see the results of your efforts. Yet, in this book, knowing your time constraints, I have digested and synthesized all of the tips and techniques into bite-sized action plans.

Pick any page, read a tip, and put it into action. In fact, if you are traveling, you can read something in Los Angeles and put it into action by the time you land in Chicago. The key is implementation.

Although everyone needs to network at their own pace, I have three main recommendations:

1. **Create your own order.** When someone asks me where to start, I say, "Anywhere." The point is to just "do it" the way you work best—which is the only way it will work for you. Pick any tip or topic and concentrate on just that one. One of my clients told me that she randomly opens a page in one of my other books and just reads that page. "Somehow I find the technique to implement something I am working on," she says. If this is the kind of inspiration you need, pick one chapter and dive in. There is no order; you create your own order as you go along.

2. **Know where you are and where you are going.** Set goals for how you want to work with new friends and business acquaintances to build a business and/or personal network.

3. **Get into the habit of networking.** Once you've learned the basics, you will feel more comfortable. You will enjoy meeting people and giving to them as much as they may give to you. Your network is your community, and you are an integral part of it. Here is an interesting thought: You are already networking in some fashion. I believe networking is a state of mind, an awareness of creating all sorts of connections and nurturing the ones you already have. Every tip in this book is timeless. Even if technology changes—yet again—the basic principles hold true. Human nature has always been the same, and networking involves people skills that have been proven over the centuries.

In this book, I give you insight into people, and then it's up to you to implement the skills you learn into your life. Technology enables the efficiency and frequency of our communications to move at lightning speed. Yet it is still the basic interpersonal, in-person techniques that are the most effective—and using these skills constantly and consistently is what makes them work.

Introduction

Networking is about giving first.

Think of the amazing power you'll gain by following the advice from this statement. You will always feel better about yourself, and you might make someone else feel better, too. This simple statement can do a lot, not only for your business, but also for your life. It goes with my other favorite saying, which my father taught me: Give without remembering and receive without forgetting.

Start right now by thinking of someone you can reach out to and help with a business lead or reference, or someone to whom you can give a simple kindness or sincere compliment. Make sure that whenever you receive anything, no matter how small, you immediately reach back and thank the other person by note, call, email, text, gift, or some combination of them.

I was recently talking with Joel, a friend and former boss, who said the following: "We know when we are coming into the world; we just don't know when we are leaving. That is why it is a good idea to be kind to each person you meet."

Or, as my wonderful dad said every day while he was on this earth and still says to me as he looks down from heaven, "Give everyone you meet a smile and a handshake."

In going through his things after he passed, my mom and I came across this list of life lessons that he had written down and always kept in his wallet:

- Listen with your inner ear. Hear what is said with the heart, rather than what is said with words.

- Listen to the concerns of others.

- Know when it is important to just listen.

- Communication is hard work.

- Hone your skills.

- State your thoughts clearly and briefly.

- Remember to smile, not scowl.

- Above all, be reasonable and understanding.

- Be friendly and enthusiastic.

- Have a sense of humor.

- Be human.

- Laugh and grin.

If you had known him, you would recognize that he lived these lessons every day, not only in his medical practice but also in his life, with whomever he came in contact.

The thought expressed by Mother Teresa that "kind words can be short and easy to speak and their echoes are truly endless" resonates with me. But how can kindness translate into business?

Whether you are aware of it or not, no matter what your responsibilities are in the organization, you are in one way or another in sales, and you will be more successful when you try to communicate your ideas when you treat everyone like your best customer. Here are some ways to do that:

- Learn where you fit into your organization. Even if you don't serve customers directly, become familiar with skills that create friendly, professional, and dependable service.

- Answering and responding to all requests quickly shows others you are dependable. Technology makes this easy.

- Create a definition of quality service that has meaning for you.

- Learn to adapt basic customer service skills to the way you treat the "customer" who works alongside you—your co-worker.

- Go the extra mile to help and take the high road. There is less traffic there.

- Courtesy is always and will always be in style.

- Always be prepared.

I hope this book encourages you to take the time to reflect and get inspired about yourself—to look back on your past successes and create a new vision for your future.

Empowerment is very attainable for each of us, as is the feeling of ownership and accomplishment.

Tom Watson, Sr., the former chairman of IBM, knew how to inspire all 67,000 of his employees, and this was before the instant technology we often take for granted today. He carried with him at all times index cards upon which he wrote pertinent things about the people he met—their family, interests, and so on—so he could always remember something personal and friendly to say to them. His kindness to his employees helped build IBM.

1

Networking Is a Mindset

When you stand in the checkout line at the grocery store, you probably do like I do and take a quick peek at whatever celebrity story the tabloids are trying to spin, avoid looking at the candy bars seductively sitting on the opposite shelves, and maybe have a casual conversation with the checkout clerk or another person in line: "How do you like that brand?" "Maybe I should try some." "Getting ready for the holidays?"

People like to chat—even introverts like me. Sometimes you drift into discussing what you do and even exchanging contact information. This casual scenario can happen on a plane, on a park bench, and even waiting to be seated in a restaurant. You make a connection, however brief, and, like a seed, it blooms into something more a year later, three years later, or even longer. I've had it happen, and you can, too. Does it mean you're manipulative or conniving? No. You are connecting. And when you practice connecting, you will find that often something good can come of it. That's what networking is all about. You come to enjoy it, do it well, and sometimes develop new relationships and opportunities.

Networking is a mindset. It is a strategy for life, a way to create lasting connections and enrich all areas of your life. Networking is 24/7. People come into your life for a reason, a season, or a lifetime.

When someone is in your life for a reason, it is usually to meet a need you have expressed. They have come to assist you through a situation, to provide you with guidance and support, to aid you physically, emotionally, or spiritually. They may even seem like a Godsend—and they are.

Then, without any wrongdoing on your part or at an inconvenient time, the relationship may come to an end. Sometimes the people you've met pass away; sometimes they walk away. Sometimes they act up and force you to take a stand. What you must realize is that your need has been met, your desire fulfilled, and their work is done. This is life, and you must realize it.

Tip 1: Networking Now Is Part of My Life

I have come to think of networking not as something that I have to do. Instead, I look at it as part of my makeup, of who I am. I think, "How can I be a resource to others, give something to them or learn from them?" They are all part of my strategic networking. This can become part of your life strategy as well, and be with you all the time. For instance, think right now about the following:

- Who can you send a note or article to that would give them an idea? Who can you just say hello to?

- What did you learn today from someone you know or someone you met or observed? (By the way, we can even learn from people we don't like or respect. They teach us what *not* to do.)

- Who can you refer today? Maybe you just spoke with a client or friend, and they are looking for a job or opportunity. Maybe you can reach out for an exploratory meeting with someone you have connected with on Facebook or LinkedIn.

Tip 2: Dedicated Networking Always (DNA)

I often say that networking is part of my DNA now. I have learned to look at how to give to others with the sheer honest passion of helping and being open. It does not take much to have this mindset, and it is amazing how opportunities come back over time.

My friend, Elliot DeBear, calls his DNA the "golf network." Here's what he has to say about this subject:

"While I did not realize it at the time, my earliest networking efforts began when I was a caddy at a local country club. The club members liked my work ethic, how I handled myself on the golf course, and my love of the game. Over time, I got to know the members and they watched me grow up. I gained trust and credibility along the way. As I started to get summer internships, and when my career as a caddy came to a close, I had developed a terrific group of relationships. A group of people who cared about my progress and wanted to see me do well.

"My first full-time job after college was at a major advertising agency, and I was recruited by a club member who was an executive at the firm. Later in life, as I started my own business, I was able to leverage many of my relationships that I had developed on the golf course. This was because of a long-standing trust developed over time. Referrals poured in because of my tremendous golf network. I saw this as a valuable lesson. Stay in touch with those who knew you when you are on your way up and find ways always to help them. Friendships were forged, and from those friendships came more opportunities. It was a win/win all around.

"Golf is my game because it requires a positive attitude, practice, patience, discretion, and a willingness to learn. However, it will work with whatever your game or passion is. Make it a part of your life."

Tip 3: The ABCs of Networking

I created this list of ABC's as a simple way to remember some tactical and strategic networking actions:

A   Take **action** with a positive **attitude**.

B   **Belong** to groups. **Build** your **brand**.

C   **Connect** with your **contacts consistently** and **cultivate** a relationship.

D   **Deliver** above expectations.

E   **Engage**, **evolve**, and **empathize**.

F   Take a **friendly** approach.

G Set **goals**. "**Go** for it." Show **gratitude**. Be **giving**.

H **Humor** and **help** go hand in hand.

I Be **interested** and have **integrity**.

J **Join** and get involved.

K **Keep** in touch and be **kind**.

L **Listen** and **learn**.

M **Motivate** yourself.

N **Niceness** pays.

O Ask **open**-ended questions. Take **opportunities**.

P **Professionalism** pays. **Practice** it.

Q Set your own **quota**.

R Be a **resource** and do your **research**.

S Be **strategic** and wear a **smile**.

T **Timing** is everything. **Trust** is key.

U **Understand** others.

V Be **versatile**.

W **Write** letters and cards.

X Do it with love, **XOXO** (or at least like).

Y Focus on "**you**"—meaning the other person you are connecting with.

Z Have a **zeal** for the possibilities of new and nurtured relationships.

Tip 4: Open Your Eyes—Networking Is All Around

Research tells us that there are at least 200 people who are already a part of your network. Get reacquainted with them. Networking is about creating and developing opportunities through meeting people and "connecting the dots" among them. The following categories of people can be the beginning of a great networking success story:

- **Customers and clients**—They are the lifeblood of your business. Build trustworthy and positive relationships with them.

- **Suppliers and external partners**—Refer them and stay on their radar screen.

- **Colleagues and co-workers**—Office pals are a powerful resource when networking. Invite a co-worker to lunch or coffee and get to know him or her better. Build your internal alliances consistently.

- **People in your profession**—Helping your competition can actually lead to greater opportunities to grow your business.

- **Alumni and former classmates**—Seize the opportunity to link up with people with whom you might want to reconnect. Linked In and Facebook are perfect for this.

- **Like-minded people**—Expand your horizons. Extracurricular activities introduce you to people with common interest and ambitions, or who share similar life experiences.

- **Neighbors**—Turn a friendly wave into an invaluable conversation. Get to know your neighbors. You can open up the door for a new opportunity.

- **Friends**—Take time to nurture and cultivate your friends. Network with them in a positive way, never with expectations.

- **Family**—Family members can be a great resource for networking opportunities. Think of how you can be helpful to those in your family.

- **People you meet serendipitously**—Be kind to unfamiliar people. Airports, grocery store lines, and waiting rooms are filled with a world of networking opportunities. Keep your ears and eyes open. I learn daily by paying attention to the universe.

Think of people you know who fit in each of these categories. The possibilities for networking are endless. Over time, as you build rapport and trust, these relationships lead to other contacts, partnerships, and opportunities.

Tip 5: Think Motivation M.A.G.I.C.

Take the following steps to continually work a bit of M.A.G.I.C. into your life:

M   What the **mind** can believe, the mind can achieve. It starts with your own self-talk. Self-talk is your inner voice, the little voice that plays in our head 24/7. Be uplifting and think about the best you have to offer. I once heard it said that depending on our self-talk, we are either in the construction or destruction business.

A   **Attitude** is everything! Our attitude is our choice, and sometimes it's a challenge to stay positive. When our personal foundation is a good attitude, it lends strength to everything else we build on it.

G   Set **goals** and go for them. Keep your eye on your dream and work hard to achieve it. Write down your goals and keep them somewhere you will see them.

I   Have **integrity** in all you do. A great reputation takes time to develop and can be destroyed in seconds. *Honesty* is the first word in the dictionary of virtues. You start by being true to yourself and making promises you know you will keep.

C   **Care** about others. Reach out to them. It is a sign of your inner strength when you take the first step to help someone. Make someone else's life a little better—it comes back to you in ways unimaginable. That gratification is sure to lift your spirits.

Steve, another self-proclaimed introvert, ran into a high-powered executive at his global financial services firm. She suggested he stop by her office to catch up. He did not think she was really serious and felt too shy and uncertain to pursue the opportunity. They ran into each other on another occasion and, again, she suggested he visit her office. Yet again he failed to visit and did not even send a thank-you note because he did not want to appear intrusive or too pushy. Later at a meeting, she joined him and a colleague, who raved about Steve's work. She replied, "Really? I can't seem get him on my calendar!"

This time he took the cue and asked for her assistant's name and immediately scheduled a meeting. When they finally met, the meeting went well, and they have continued a regular dialogue since. Now Steve is able to bring his ideas to one of the highest levels of the firm.

What did he realize from this experience? Follow up immediately, always send a thank-you note, and do not "self-negotiate" one's way out of an opportunity to make a connection.

Have a goal and an action plan for every encounter. This is a huge advantage for someone with a consistent networking-aware mind. You'll be prepared and ready to follow up easily and efficiently. I leave my home daily with a specific goal for meeting or nurturing my working network and for each meeting I have planned. I am then ready to follow up with every serendipitous encounter, as well as those I have planned in advance. If you don't know where you are going, any road will take you there. Set a positive intention daily to build and nurture your network.

Tip 6: Networking Becomes Comfortable Over Time

Networking is now more comfortable to me. It was not always so, until I realized that it is just a way of maintaining good connections with people. Now I see many opportunities that unfold when I have my ears, eyes, and mind open. Just like a parachute, they all work better when open. Think of each person you meet as a friend, client, prospect, or someone who could be one of these over time.

Tip 7: Opportunities Are Everywhere

Too often opportunities arrive disguised, and you might neglect to take the action step. Instead of saying to yourself, "I wish," "I will," "I want," or "I should," replace this with "Do it now instead of tomorrow."

A double opportunity recently developed from a speech I gave at a Chamber of Commerce meeting ten years ago. I received an email from a global organization asking me to present at an upcoming meeting. When I found out who referred me, I reached out to the managing director of the firm, whom I had not met, from the Chamber of Commerce meeting and said thank you for the recommendation to his global association. Tony Torchia of RotenbergMeril was stunned that I called to thank him since we had never actually met. This was ten years later. We did finally meet when I presented, and afterward I wanted to take him to lunch to say thank you. We had a lovely lunch, and he invited two colleagues. The "thank-you" lunch turned out to be a sales opportunity and another project. Double tip on this opportunity. Always find out your first source of any referral and say thank you, and then follow up again with either a coffee or lunch. You never know what will develop unless you reach out.

I love when people reach out to me because it always proves to be some type of opportunity. A year ago, I received an email from a 16-year-old high school student named Nicole, who contacted me to learn how to network in high school to maximize her experience and start to prepare for college. I was impressed with her, and we have stayed in touch on and off. Just last month, Nicole reached out again since her family moved to Texas and she now wanted to know how to get involved in psychology clubs—again, to get herself prepared for college. I asked Nicole how she knew to initially reach out to me. It turns out that her father was one of my drivers from a car service I use to go to the airport. He and I talked one day during a ride, and he told me about his very bright and ambitious daughter. I told him to have her reach out to me and I would try to help her—and she actually did.

Remember to reach out to people and follow up.

Tip 8: An Exercise in Attitude

Try this attitude exercise. Great client service requires you to be thoughtful and appreciative throughout the business development process. Clients assume that you will thank them after you have done business. Here are a few "attitude of gratitude" thoughts to deliver in all your business relationships:

- **Go beyond surface information.** Learn as much as you can about all your contacts and connections.

- **You must have "heart."** People make decisions with both their head and heart. Keep feelings in mind. It is the personal relationship that keeps you in good graces.

- **Give thanks for bad news as well as good.** We usually celebrate successful wins and let clients know how much their business means to us. Yet when we lose an order or a piece of business, we don't. We may feel paralyzed by the loss. Even with a rejection, show appreciation by sending a note of thanks for their time and consideration. You may be surprised by the outcome.

Tip 9: Act on Things Immediately

As an effective time manager, I act on things immediately because I know that tomorrow I will have ten more things I must do. Take things step-by-step, and do what you say you will as part of your brand building. This way, you will be known for following up and following through.

I'll never forget the voice mail message I received from a financial advisor named Michelle who had enjoyed my first book on networking and said that she had learned a lot of things that she had never considered before. She was so surprised that I called her back—yet follow-up is one of the best practices of essential networking. Over time, she introduced me to a woman named Annmarie Woods of Mainstay Investments. We met and started working together later and became great friends. Over the years, from that one phone call and follow-up, I have worked with many people at Annmarie's firm and with other colleagues who left to join other firms. It is *all* about the follow-up.

Tip 10: Manage Your Time

Get up ten minutes early and be productive right away. You'll be surprised to discover how much time you have created through those extra minutes during which you can start a project, connect online, write a handwritten note to someone in your network, read a book, or do some exercise.

Ask yourself the following questions:

- How much of my time is spent with clients or people in my network?

- Do I confirm appointments?

- Is my paperwork done completely and correctly?

- Do I plan and practice my presentations in advance?

- Am I willing to meet with people at their convenience instead of mine?

- Do I frequently take productive coffee and lunch meetings with the people in my network?

Help yourself by performing the following tasks:

- List a couple ways you don't use your time as effectively as you could.

- Explain how you could be more productive with your time.

Don't get caught up in the Five Emotional Time Wasters: indecision, guilt, worry, perfectionism, and procrastination. Time is your best friend and also your biggest enemy. It keeps moving, so use it wisely. Sometimes you have to slow down to follow up properly. Don't multitask. When you do two things at once, it is hard to do either very well. Direct your attention and concentration toward the moment and the task at hand. It will be hard at first, yet as you complete each task, it will go faster, and you won't have to stop and go back to correct the mistakes that happen when you try doing several things at once. Don't believe me? Think of the last time you were on the phone while checking email at the same time. Were you able to answer and respond to each task efficiently and with the attention it deserved? Also, when someone steps into your office or meets with you, stop what you are doing and pay attention. Here is a tip: I always say, "How much time do we need right now?"

Tip 11: Things to Do

Keep your "to-do" list short and do the items on it. This way, you will have a sense of accomplishment. I keep my list on an app on my phone. We all have fantastic systems right in our hand to help us keep track of things. Some items can and will be put on hold. I like to keep my list short and to the point.

Set aside chunks of time to do the tasks. Batch your emails, calls, texts, and LinkedIn communications and even your note-writing time. It is amazing what you can accomplish in only 10 to 15 minutes of productive time. I have known people who have mastered a new language by studying only 15 minutes a day consistently over time. Until you have done it, don't disbelieve it!

Here are my friend Lawrence Peters' thoughts about the courtesy of replying to an email:

> "In our fast-paced world, often the reality is that people don't reply and leave us hanging. Take the time to quickly hit Reply and at least give a status if you don't have the full information. Sometimes it is easier to pick up the phone—the main goal is that if someone requires an answer, reply to them as soon as you can."

Tip 12: Time Action Tips to Do Now

1. Write daily, *specific, measurable outcomes* you want to achieve.

2. Every day review top projects and what can be done to move them closer to fruition.

3. Set your priorities—what is urgent and needs to be done now?

4. Periodically, ask yourself, "Is what I am doing now the most important thing I can be doing at this time?"

5. Establish place habits. "A place for everything and everything in its place." It keeps you organized.

6. Create systems for forms, check lists, and repetitive tasks. Technology makes this easy.

7. Complete what you start. Leave nothing unfinished.

8. One hour of planning will save three hours of execution.

9. Develop a "do it now" approach. *Eliminate indecision.*

10. Pre-plan each week and allocate time to perform necessary functions.

11. At the end of each day, create a carry-over list of items that were not accomplished. Keep your time log and list going so you can refer back to the undone items.

12. Regularly analyze your use of time. Adapt and adjust when required to improve your efficiency and productivity.

Tip 13: It's Not Who You Know, It's Who You Thank

Although an entire industry has developed around motivating people through appreciation, it ultimately boils down to what our parents taught us: Say "thank you" to everyone. This may seem like simple etiquette, yet it is amazing what saying thank you can do for your business and personal relationships. When we express our appreciation to clients, co-workers, employees, and friends, their attitudes are positively affected, and positive attitudes impact business and personal success.

An effective way to say thank you is with a gift, because not only is it an expression of gratitude, but it also serves as a reminder, keeping you in the thoughts of others so that they will contact you again. At the end of my training seminars and presentations, I like to stay in touch with the people who I have connected with. One way I do that is to send a small gift right after the program, and then follow up at least every three months with tokens of appreciation to keep my name in front of them.

One year, my holiday thank-you gift to many of my clients and business friends was a light bulb-shaped glass filled with mints, imprinted with, "A world of thanks," and it included my name. People can continually refill and use the bulb, and I often still see it on people's desks. It does have a long shelf life.

Other people require a more personalized thank you. In many cases, I take the time to find gifts that fit specific interests. For instance, I know that one client is a cat lover, so I found a wonderful crystal cat for him. Another client loves a certain restaurant, and I gave her a gift certificate. The point is to consider what people will appreciate most.

Tip 14: Face Problems with Innovation

Here's an exercise for thinking "innovation" when facing a challenge:

1. Replace the word *problem* with the word *challenge* in your life.

2. Define what the challenge is. (For instance, I have a prospect who keeps putting off our appointment.)

3. Prepare three suggestions to meet the challenge.

4. Write down what part of the challenge you can affect and what part you can't.

5. Prepare an action plan to meet the challenge. (For instance, I can change the place of the appointment and meet the prospect for lunch; I can show up at the appointed time no matter what and say that I forgot he had rescheduled; I can show up unexpectedly and say I was in the neighborhood; I can put off the next appointment, putting the control back in my hands.)

6. Put the plan into action.

Tip 15: Never Forget Those Who Help You

Remembering those who help you is the life blood of true networking and relationships. As my good friend James Palazza (one of the world's best salespeople and relationship builders) says, "I live by this rule. Always remember those who go out of their way for you."

2

Positioning Yourself and Creating Your Brand

As I sit in Starbucks and watch a city block of people clamoring to come inside when there are three other coffee shops on the next block, I wonder, "Why am I here?" The coffee is strong and expensive, yet it is the aura and the mystique of the brand that brings me back. The other day when shopping at my favorite "local" Whole Foods—which is ten city blocks from me—I considered why there are always droves of people there. It is the customer experience of being there—great food, conveniently and creatively displayed. Yet again, the brand drew me in.

It reminds me of when I heard the founder of JetBlue speaking at a conference. He talked about how they built their brand on flawless execution and taking care of the customer. Like any organization, they faced many challenges over the years—and still do. As he spoke at the conference, I heard someone say, "He came here to speak to this group for free." I thought about that comment. Here he was talking in front of a group of 200 executives about the airline's customer service. He gave everyone a JetBlue cap, and he shared different stories based on his mantra of taking care of the customer. He was fabulous. Each person in that room was talking about his speech—and JetBlue—when they left, praising it to everyone in sight. I know I did! Much of the new business JetBlue, Starbucks, and Whole Foods get is from the buzz created from people talking to each other—in other words, networking! So, did the CEO really speak for free?

Your brand is who you are and what people think about when they hear your name—it's very much like the "customer experience" of life. It is not just how you look to yourself, it is how you look to others. It is painting in someone's mind a word picture of yourself—and how you create that image. For instance, what do you envision from the following example?

My friend Vicky Amon is an amazing chef, though cooking is her hobby, not her profession. When I asked her one night what she was preparing for dinner, instead of saying the plain and obvious, she told me, "You can have fish, corn, and salad for dinner—or, you can have pistachio-encrusted tilapia, fresh corn on the cob with garlic/parsley butter, and a salad of Farmer's Market romaine, sliced avocado, Parmesan croutons, pine nuts, and dried cranberries with a Dijon Caesar dressing."

Which would you prefer? Again, it is all in the presentation and the articulation. How would *you* create you? Think now about your own branding as you network. Here is how to get started:

1. Write down your unique selling points (USPs). We all have them.

2. Define what makes you "unique." In my case, it is, "I follow-up fast and efficiently."

3. Consider your positioning strategy (that is, how you wish to be perceived). How do you like to be positioned in the minds of others?

4. Consider how you "live" your brand. (You must "walk your talk," so to speak.)

5. Consider what people think of when they hear your name.

Put together your positioning statement and continually upgrade it. It should answer the following questions:

- Who are you?

- What business are you in? What business do you *want* to be in?

- Whom do you serve?

- Who is your competition?

- How do you differentiate yourself?

- What unique benefit do you provide so that someone will say, "You are the one for me on this project"?

Remember:

- A **position** is how you are perceived in the minds of others.

- A **positioning statement** expresses how you wish to be perceived.

Tip 1: The Top-Ten Cs of a Strong Personal Brand

1. **Correct**—A strong personal brand is accurate and authentic. So be true to yourself and your brand will shine.

2. **Concise**—A strong personal brand can be described in one or two sentences. Distill your brand qualities into a brief statement that describes your unique promise of value.

3. **Clear**—A strong personal brand is about what it is and what it is not. Make two lists describing what's on and off brand for you.

4. **Consistent**—A strong personal brand is always the same. It is your promise of value to your customers, clients, managers, peers, and so on.

5. **Constant**—A strong personal brand is always there, visible and available. It doesn't go into hiding.

6. **Compelling**—A strong personal brand is appropriate and interesting to your target audience. It is relevant.

7. **Clever**—A strong personal brand is highly differentiated and unique. It creates interest among your target market and separates you from others with similar skills and abilities.

8. **Connected**—A strong personal brand is part of the appropriate communities. This means having a network of partners, colleagues, and customers.

9. **Committed**—A strong personal brand is in it for the long haul.

10. **Current**—A strong personal brand is based on today, with room to evolve for tomorrow. Be fresh and consistently updating.

Tip 2: Your Personal Brand Statement—What People Think of When They Think of You

When you make your introduction to a new contact, does your personal brand statement (PBS) meet these requirements?

1. **Hearing it makes people go "WOW!"** Providing good or excellent service is not enough these days. If you want to create a livelihood from your business (in other words, it's not just a hobby), then you need to stand out from the crowd. Clients are attracted to people who make them go "WOW!" Make what you say action oriented and a benefit of what you do.

2. **It's only one breath long.** You should be able to say your personal brand statement in one "out breath." This is like creating a sound bite that people can easily remember. Test it: Can the other person repeat back to you what you said, verbatim? "I help people retire comfortably and with dignity."

3. **It clearly states practical benefits.** The practical benefits of what you are should be clear or at least clearly implied.

4. **It reflects your own personality.** Your PBS should be uniquely identifiable with you. If any one of your friends or acquaintances can say the same statement about themselves in the same way as you, then you need to inject more of you in your statement. Stay away from the generic (for example, "I help you increase your profits"). Your personality can be projected in how you phrase your statement, in the words you use, your tone of voice, and so on.

5. **It projects confidence and energy.** Your PBS should roll off your tongue easily, without tripping. You must be able to project it.

6. **It gives enough to cause people to ask for more.** Your PBS is a "teaser" to start a dialogue with your customer.

7. **It fits with who you are; it is real and grounded.** Going beyond reflecting your personality, your PBS basically describes how you express your personal mission in the physical world, your role in the world. Use "I" phrasing instead of trying to create the

impression that you're something bigger or other than who you are. (This is a tendency especially with self-employed people.)

8. **It can be made into an even shorter form.** Your PBS should be almost like a slogan, brand, or theme.

9. **It can change with time.** Your PBS evolves with time, reflecting what you are passionate about at the moment. You can continually change it.

10. **It can be repeated easily by others.** The ultimate success of a PBS is how well it creates buzz or word of mouth. If your PBS meets all of the preceding requirements, people will accurately talk about who you are and what you offer, thus triggering the attraction forces that work so well.

Tip 3: Your Personal Presentation

Here are some tips on your presentation—keep in mind you are "always presenting to someone":

- Limit your own talking.
- Listen to the other with your eyes and ears.
- Ask open-ended questions.
- Hold your thoughts—don't interrupt.
- Use positive interjections.
- Use persuasive, positive selling words.

Tip 4: I Can't Hear You Because What I See Is Louder

We've been taught "never judge a book by its cover," yet we still do! It may be unfair to judge someone in a matter of minutes, yet that is sometimes all we have. Although how we dress doesn't change how smart we are, or how thoughtful, it does affect other people's opinions of us. Moreover, these opinions can affect our career advancement. Start to use your image as a tool.

How people are treated often depends on the first impression they give to others. Life is one constant change. World events, fashion, and ideas always change, so we must learn to keep changing. This is why it is important to look at ourselves objectively and keep abreast of what is right and needs improvement about our appearance. We usually feel better about ourselves when we make an effort to look our very best and communicate in a way that puts us in the best possible light.

Tip 5: The Power You Hold

The first thing anyone notices when you walk into a room is the image you project. Are they right about you? Ask yourself the following questions:

- How would you describe yourself?

- Does your appearance communicate to others the message you want to convey?

- How important is it to you to present a positive and professional image as you represent your company?

- As you develop your communication skills and image, how might your career benefit?

- In stressful situations, what happens to your image, your first impressions, and your professional presence?

- What communication situations seem to make you uncomfortable? Public speaking? Interviews?

The more objectively you think about and respond to these questions, the more effectively you will be able to manage and upgrade your personal and professional growth.

Here are some quick tips to keep in mind as you work past your first impression to the second one, which begins when you start to talk with someone:

- Be pleasant. Your smile is a great opener.

- Talk and act confidently. Confidence inspires confidence.

- Be truthful and sincere. It goes with confidence.

- Be enthusiastic. It's contagious.

It has been said that the impression you make in the first 30 seconds can impact and be more important than anything you do or say in the next 30 minutes.

My friend Karen Visconti, who I met in a professional class 16 years ago, told me her boss describes her in three words: prepared, professional, and passionate. This totally describes her.

Tip 6: Self-Image

Always stay true to yourself. Only compete with yourself—that is enough. Set your goals high and achievable and strive for new and better things as they relate to your life and business. Yet, know what you can and will do to achieve what you set out to do. This is where the work comes in and meets up with opportunity.

Be who you are to yourself. Be creative and think, "How do I maintain my individuality at the company or in my business?" Individuality is key—avoid a "cookie-cutter" mentality.

Tip 7: Become the "Facilitator"— Introduce Others

Find a way to take on the Facilitator role. My friend John is a master at this. He walks around a company meeting and brings people together. He knows these people—or at least something about them—and their work and their department or region. As he would tell you, he is rather shy and introverted, yet he has pushed himself to learn more about people and take on this role to also enhance his internal company networking.

Tip 8: A Quick Self-Introduction for Every Event

Depending on your audience, situation, or environment, you need to introduce yourself in different ways. Here are a couple examples:

- At an industry event, for instance, I might say, "I take the anxiety out of networking and public speaking." And then as someone looks at me, I turn to them and say, "And what do you do?" They may have forgotten that they asked me what I do and just tell me what they do. I always find a way to connect the dots back to me when there is an interest.

- If someone says, "I am an attorney at a large corporate firm," I might respond with this: "I teach attorneys 'rainmaking' skills so that they can get their points across simply and persuasively and attain new business."

I strive to set goals and find new ways to describe what I do and the benefits I can provide each person I connect with *after* I learn what they do. Does it always work? No. However, it is great practice. We find ourselves in situations every day where we can test out new sound bites. Think of a way to introduce yourself at the deli, the health club, a new event, a cocktail party, a school meeting. Just don't say your title at first; instead, give the action and benefit grabbers of what you do.

Tip 9: Always Improve and Refine Your Skills

How do I continually refine my skills, my surroundings—the biggest aspect of these being the room for self-improvement? Strive for the next big thing.

I recently joined a new club to take clients to lunches and dinners and to provide a place for expanding my social network. I have also gotten involved in two other charitable associations. Not only do I feel that I am giving back to others, I am also enhancing my knowledge by meeting new people from whom I continually learn.

Whatever you do, find the opportunity to always be learning and observing others. Sometimes, instead of reading a magazine, I look at other people to see what they are wearing, how they are putting themselves together, how they speak, and what trends they are discussing. It is almost like treating the world as a "book without borders," each page written with your experiences.

Tip 10: Change Your Scenery

Changing your scenery does not mean moving; it just means changing one thing about your routine or status quo. Get out of your networking comfort zone. Go somewhere different—take a day trip to a museum, volunteer at a hospital, take a class on something that intrigues you yet is not in your "core business" life. Observe and connect with the other people you meet along the way. You never know what you'll learn from each and every walk of life, yet you will be enriched for it. As you learn from each person you connect with, you learn about different topics and subjects. I continually have an array of small talk topics to pick from in every conversation.

Tip 11: Start "Client-Telling"

Take five of your clients, contacts, friends, or associates to lunch. Introduce each to the other and create connections for the pure synergy of having other bright and interesting people meet each other. What you invest in this "event" will come back to you many times over the years—with all types of surprising and interesting opportunities.

I always think of the people first and how they might learn something from the others there—and then what they will contribute by being there. Whenever I do this, it is fun, extremely interactive, and rewarding. It is a wonderful way for me to continually nurture my network.

Tip 12: Words to Live By

Think of the following as your daily mantras:

- Feel you deserve the best.
- Develop strong habits.
- Get uncluttered and organized—streamline things.
- Create your own rituals.

My friend Bob Lamb is now an entrepreneur after working in corporate America for many years. In order to feel he is "totally at work," he makes sure to get up early every morning and go to mass before starting his day. He accomplishes two things: He gets up and dressed and goes somewhere to create a routine and structure for his day, and he goes to worship first thing in the morning and comes back to his office inspired and ready to go.

What is your routine, and how do you prepare for each and every new day? What goals do you set and how do you measure them?

Tip 13: Reinvent Yourself

I often ask myself the following question: "In the grocery store of life, why would someone pick me off the crowded shelf—am I new and improved, repackaged?"

Here is how a friend of mine, Jeannette Paladino, Writer-in-Chief at Write Speak Sell, started her own reinvention of her career:

> "When I left my last job in the business world, I had no idea that social media would become my beat. I had held senior marketing communications positions with major companies and PR agencies. But if you believe in serendipity, then you will appreciate that my world changed when a friend mentioned to me that she had taken a blogging course. It sounded interesting, so I signed up. I became totally engrossed in this new world of social media. At first, it was more of a hobby. I was challenged to learn something new—so I took courses, did a lot of reading, and rebranded myself as a social media writer, blogger, and project manager. Before you know it, I had a business. It's never too late to learn new skills. No matter what your age or background, try something new. Feed that passion you always had for painting, or acting, or whatever. Go for it!"

Reinvention is like change: Many folks fear change. It can be both scary and exhilarating. Change is your only constant, however, so do something today a little different—reach out of your comfort zone and see new results while learning opportunities each step of the way.

Tip 14: Rethink Everything You Do

Check and double-check. More opportunities are ruined through careless mistakes or by trying to do too much at once without focus.

Create a check list. I have different ones for events and work and constantly upgrade and refine them. Start simple, though, and just have one. For example, say you are going to an industry event today:

- Set a goal to meet and connect with two or three people.

- Be specific. Write out your goal for the event or meeting.

- Have your "elevator intro" so practiced that it rolls off your tongue—for that particular audience.

- Have your tangible and intangible toolkits with you and ready to go, including the following:

  - The research you've done before the event

  - Eye contact—look at someone as if that person is the only one in the room

  - Ears open and ready to *listen*—turn off other "volume" in your head

  - Proper body language and appearance

  - A smile

  - All equipment turned off

  - Business cards or your smartphone handy to exchange information

  - Small paper and pen portfolio to write notes

  - A "small talk" notebook that contains anecdotes to stimulate conversation

  - Grooming essentials

  - Business card cases—one for your cards and one for the ones you collect

- Pack your note cards/stationery with stamps so you are ready to write your thank-you notes.

I pull out this check list before every event. I always want to be 120-percent prepared. Remember, your most important power is the power of thought.

Tip 15: Your Image Collection

Imagine that a photo was taken of you every time you met another person during the day. Put together a mental photo album of all these pictures of you—this is your "image collection." Ask yourself what you "see" about yourself with these questions:

- Do I come across as articulate, persuasive, and sure of myself?

- Do I appear trustworthy?

- Do I have a "winning image"?

Research tells us the following make for a favorable first impression:

- Being a good listener

- Having a nice appearance

- Commenting back to the person on something they said to show interest

- The ability to create a rapport

3

Creating Connections

reating connections with others is one of the key components of essential networking. It is the first step in expanding and deepening your universal network. You have to start by taking the action step and creating the first step from upon which you will start to build, grow, and expand your network.

Tip 1: Be Curious at Work

"Are you a sports fan?" I asked the man on the shuttle between Boston and New York. He was reading a book about the Yankees versus Red Sox—always a great conversation opener anywhere on the East Coast. I then ordered the book on Amazon. Whether you have the hard copy or you read on your tablet, having a book with you at all times could be a conversation starter. You never know.

Be attentive at lectures, meetings, and associations where you can learn a lot from the speaker. I remember attending a dinner years ago where the most interesting panelist was Nick Risom. When the event ended, I just walked right up and said, "Thank you so much for enlightening me about the insurance world. May I have your card?"

Later, I followed up with a note and did my research online to learn more about Nick. He has since become my insurance broker, friend, and a great source of referrals.

Walk by someone's office or cubicle and find something to comment on to start a conversation. Be curious at work.

Tip 2: Notice People and Things About Them, and Reach Out

Be curious in life. When I see something that is interesting—a piece of jewelry or a gadget, I might say, "Tell me the story about your _____."

In fact, I did this with a person I met who is in the diamond business. He was wearing the most amazing watch at breakfast and I asked him about it. It turns out that he "won" the watch by purchasing raffle tickets for a charity. "I'd never won anything before!" he said, as we discussed the charity with which he is now deeply involved. It opened an entirely new area for our conversations as we shared information. Now I am on the lookout for more information for him in my list of interests so that I can send it to him as a much appreciated way to stay on his radar screen.

What happened in this instance? First, I learned something new about him, then I got an education about his favorite charity, and finally I found a way to stay in touch with him by noting his interests and being alert for more information for him about those interests. When you ask people—even those you know well—about themselves, you find new things, topics, and interests to file away and share with them when "life" presents them. That is why I always collect what I call "vital information." You never know when, how, and to whom you can pass this information along and brighten their day.

Reach out—and be curious.

Tip 3: Show Others You Value Them

What a gift when we show appreciation to others and let them know they are important to us. Taking the time to remember important things and interests about them can be taken as the highest compliment:

- Use people's names. Everyone likes to hear their name and to know that you are interested enough to remember it. Also, be sure to spell it correctly. I know people who spell their name "Scot," "Ric," "Kathee," and "Jon."

- Acknowledge their presence. Something as simple as, "Good morning. How are you, Mary? I missed you at today's meeting," can be a way to show someone you are aware of their existence.

- Remember small details about people. To them it is not small and is a huge connector.

- Remember people's birthdays, anniversaries, graduations, and other significant occasions by sending a card or gift or by connecting electronically or by telephone. (If you are really close and connected, you can do this for the members of their families as well.) People are often impressed when someone remembers occasions that are special to them. I remember because I write them down and store them in my contact management system. I record this information from my phone into my database. Technology makes this easy.

- Let people know you are available to help them in some way. Use your expertise to help others (within acceptable boundaries and parameters).

- Be in the moment when speaking to people. This means listening closely to what is and is not said, as well as absorbing body language when face-to-face. Letting someone know you are truly in the moment when you speak with them can be manifested by small acknowledgments of their personality, work, hobby, and so on.

- Give proper credit. Giving credit where credit is due is important to valuing someone. It also raises your credibility in their eyes.

- Be fair, regardless of someone's status or position. Treating people fairly means enforcing the rules of civility for everyone all the time.

- Be equitable. Playing favorites because it suits your agenda or circumstance is devaluating to the receiver and to observers. Everyone has importance and deserves respect.

Tip 4: F.A.C.E. Tip

Face-to-face connections are sometimes overshadowed by technology. Make it a point to create "face" time (or personal time) with your contacts. Here is what that means to me:

F Be **friendly**. When you start any interaction with strong eye contact, you automatically connect and rapport begins.

A **Adapt** to the other's surroundings. Look around when in someone's office—you can learn a lot. (Just make sure it is that person's office!) Maybe you recognize a book you've read on their shelf, or you learn you are both tennis players. Use these and other shared interests as a conversation starter.

C **Connect** and think of questions that will help you understand the person better. Do your homework—look at their LinkedIn profile. Google them. Just be prepared. We all feel more comfortable with a person who seems to have a genuine interest in us and wants to build rapport and trust.

E Know when to **exit**. Take the lead to finish the meeting and thank the person for their time. No one will fault you for ending a meeting early. Less is more, and you may be invited back.

Tip 5: Don't Waste Opportunities to Connect

I was having dinner at a new restaurant with my friend and former boss, Rick Botthof, in a suburb of Chicago. The manager came around to introduce himself and see how our dinner was. He asked if we were from the area. Rick said he was; I said I was visiting on business from New York. He immediately shifted his attention to Rick, trying to find out about his business and whether he would refer colleagues to the restaurant. He ignored me and the possibility that I might be the visiting president of a large company who could refer my sizeable Chicago staff to his restaurant, or that I might be addressing more than 200 people from the area on networking and creating relationships the next day— which I was. What a mistake on his part!

To add fuel to the fire, before he walked away, he gave Rick his card and said to him, but not me, "Feel free to call me." If he had been savvier and truly interested in business development, he would have taken both of our cards and then dropped each of us a note, saying, "Thank you for your visit, hope you enjoyed it, and please come back." We would both have recommended his restaurant had he made this small gesture. Instead, I won't mention its name. No buzz created from this neglected patron. This may seem like a small thing, yet I looked at it as a wasted opportunity.

Tip 6: Never Assume

We all know what happens when we assume. This is another reason I believe in biting one's tongue and waiting before speaking. You could lose a sale, talk yourself out of something already sold, or make a fool of yourself.

Tip 7: Learn by Listening—and Don't Talk Just to Talk

A man I respect told me his philosophy about the power of the tongue. He cites a passage in the New Testament that describes the effect our little tongues have on our lives. He tells the story this way:

> "Take ships, for example. Although they are so large and are driven by strong winds, they are steered where the pilot wants to go by a very small rudder. Likewise, the tongue is a small part of the body, but makes great boasts. Consider what a great forest is set on fire by a small spark."

Think of this before saying something without considering the repercussions of what and how it will affect someone else. We can all go to school on this thought every day of our lives and learn valuable lessons about creating a better and sweeter environment—with thoughtful tongues.

Tip 8: Become a Better Listener

The Talmud says that "the highest form of wisdom is kindness." Sometimes the kindest thing you can do for someone who is troubled is to listen. Death and life are in the power of the tongue. Here are some tips on being a better listener:

- Ask questions.
- Slow down your "thinking rate." We think at 500 words a minute and talk at 150. That's why our minds wander. Stay focused.

- Listen for the theme. Get the key issues.

- Identify key words and use them as memory aids and stimulators (for example, something you remember easily, such as where someone is from or where they work).

- Rearrange the information that you hear. Organize it in a way that is logical for you.

- Take notes. You talk to many people, so you have to write things down to remember everything. Keep refining your note-taking skills. This may sound simple, but the challenge is in the execution.

- "Create value with every contact, and your business will live forever," says my friend Bill.

Tip 9: Work on Remembering Names

Remembering names is hard, especially at a trade show where you're meeting many people at once. Here are some easy steps for remembering:

1. When you meet someone, look them in the eye and keep your eye contact while you are talking.

2. When they mention their name, repeat it out loud, "Hi, Tom, it's great to meet you." (What you're doing is making them feel good by using their name, and it's also going into your memory bank through repetition. This also forces you to really listen. Just mention their name once or twice—not more.)

3. Form some type of association about them. Maybe they have the same name as a friend, or their name rhymes with something. We remember in pictures, and this will help your mind paint a word picture.

4. Erase this phrase from your mind: "I'm no good at remembering names." Replace it with "I'm getting better at remembering names." What the mind hears internally, it remembers.

Tip 10: If You Put Your Foot in Your Mouth, Make Sure You Are Wearing Nice Shoes!

What a reminder to me! We have all put our foot in our mouth, so be careful to "bite your tongue" the next time you even think it could be in error.

I was speaking to a group of people and happened to mention the name of someone I had worked with. Even though I was saying something nice, I realized that it is never a good idea to name drop. To make the matter worse, in my mind, I asked the group if anyone knew this person. When I thought about it later, I realized I probably offended some people, and in the future I would "zip it" when it comes to mentioning specific names—unless I have total permission to do so! I even have a sign in my office that says, "The most successful people have teeth marks on their tongue." I should have re-read it that day.

Tip 11: Create Great Connections Between Your Contacts

Think of those you like, trust, know, and respect. Who among them might have synergy? Ask those with potential connections for permission first; then take the action step of introducing them by note, email, social media, or telephone call. Then step away and let them take the next steps. Never keep score. Do this for the sake of expanding the networks and referral and relationship sources of your owned valued contacts. One person told me he heard that "making connections is like a chess game." He likes thinking of who would be good to know each other, and he bases it purely on trust, respect, and possible synergy.

The following example is from my colleague JoAnn, who explains how she created a great connection:

> "A client of mine was interviewing for a job at the company of another client. Both clients were very close friends, and although they did not know each other, I knew that they would align both personally and professionally. They were both intelligent, kind, and passionate.

"I reached out to the client at the prospective company—Client A—and asked her to put in a good word for Client B. She did so and sent a lovely note and said that any person about whom I raved was good enough to work at their company. (A very kind endorsement.) The email was extensive and elaborate and glowing. It went to the senior-most person doing the interviewing.

"Client B did interview and ultimately received the job. She felt that the email from Client A helped enormously.

"I was then moved off of both businesses to take on a new assignment prior to Client B's start date. Client A and Client B became friends professionally and personally—they adored and raved about each other from the instant they met. They felt as though they were friends before they started, which led to terrific collaboration on the businesses.

"When I was moved back onto Client A's business, they both became my clients again and we still live happily ever after today. We call it our sorority."

Tip 12: Before You Contact Someone to Whom You've Been Referred, Check with the Person Who Referred You

Learn something personal about a person to whom you've been referred from the person who referred you. This way, you'll have a much more gracious way to engage this new person in conversation. Besides, you'll be making two people feel great at the onset—the new person you are connecting with and the person who referred you!

Tip 13: Perform Random Acts of Kindness

Doing something kind makes you feel great and like a good person—so just to do it. Here are some things I like to do that you may consider doing, too:

- When you pay your toll at the toll booth, pay for the person behind you.

- When you get on your city bus or train, pay for the person behind you who looks like they are having a bad day.

Just don't let the recipients of your kindness know it came from you. The point is to do it just to make someone else feel good—as a surprise.

One time while in Germany, I was having lunch with my friend Jon Lambert (who is now looking down from heaven) when we saw a group of soldiers who were on leave and having some sort of a gathering. Before we left our meal, Jon said to the manager, "I would like to pay for all of them, but don't tell them, please." There were 25 of them! When we were leaving, however, the soldiers caught up with us. The smiles, hugs, and pure gratitude were, as my friend Jon said, "worth their total weight in gold and many times the cost of the lunch!"

Another time, as I was leaving the hairdressers, it started pouring down rain. I always carry an umbrella with me and sometimes two, but the woman next to me didn't have one and had to get to a meeting. I turned to her as I was walking to my car and said, "Here you go, and you can give it to someone else when they need an umbrella!"

Make someone else feel good—it comes back to you!

Tip 14: Clothes Make the Opportunity

Walking into a cocktail party, I saw a Wall Street executive who was wearing the same outfit that I had on. I walked over to her and said, "Excuse me, I want to compliment you on your incredible taste in clothes!" She responded by saying how much she appreciated my sense of humor. After the event, I sent her a note and the card of my personal salesperson, Don Klein, at the designer St. John Boutique if she was ever interested.

The net(working) result was that the boutique got some new business, and Don was happy. I now get invited to more of their store events, and I made a new connection.

So, ladies, if you are ever wearing the same outfit or even the same designer as another person at an event, don't despair—turn it into an opportunity to connect.

Tip 15: Networking Domino Effect

I met Scott, who is now my friend, at a conference. We stayed in touch. I introduced him to a group as a speaker and then to a radio show. He has now published his own book. Just being nice, from one person to another. Keep the process going with your friends and contacts. It is the networking domino effect.

Tip 16: Say Thank You—Even if You Didn't Get the Business

Next time you might get the job! Remember, the thank-you after a rejection goes a long way. You will be remembered as a class act.

Tip 17: Reconnect with Four People a Week

This week, try reaching out to a client or prospect you've been out of touch with—a former business colleague, a friend from the past, or a current friend you haven't spoken with for a while. Catch up, update your notes, and be ready to reconnect.

Tip 18: Determine Who You Would Like to Meet

Make a list of key people you'd like to meet in your industry or profession. Determine what organizations and places they go to and find ways to connect with them. Reach out to someone you do know and ask if they would write a letter of recommendation on your behalf—you can even offer to save them the work by writing it first and asking for their comments and edits. If you can conceive it, you can achieve it. This is popular on LinkedIn.

You be sure to do the heavy lifting first.

Tip 19: Join Civic, Industry, and Professional Groups

Research and join a civic, industry, advocacy, or professional group. Go to two meetings, meet two people, and set up two follow-up meetings—before you make your decision to join. This is my "2-2-2 Strategy." It works every time. My theory: It is quality not quantity that counts.

Join for the sake of giving, not getting. You will get a lot back over time. Write down now a couple groups you are interested in and make the calls to get started. Once you are in a group, volunteer, write an article, or join a committee. Take the action to become known in your organizations of choice. Results will happen.

Tip 20: Change the Way You Look at Things

When you change the way you look at things, the things you look at change. I read this years ago and it is indelible in my mind—think forward and positive.

Tip 21: Follow Your Interests

Take a class, join a health club, or go on a different type of vacation. I have now gone on African safaris, trips to Russia and India, and many others. Be adventurous in your own way. Remember, you need like-minded people in your network. Bonds will develop, and you will create connections that you otherwise may not have made. From my African adventure, I met a woman who was extremely successful in California. She suggested I join the Rotary Club. At first, I put her suggestion on hold because I felt I belonged to too many things. However, as life would have it, I was asked to speak at the local Rotary. I did join and have made amazing friends and contacts.

Tip 22: Action Tips to Think About

Think about the people you come across in meetings, during sales calls, or in a registration line at conferences. Everyone has the potential to be a contact. More importantly, the golden rule for networking is, instead of looking at networking as getting something from other people, think of how you can be a resource for them. Think about what you can learn from them and give to them.

Get out your hoe and seed bag. Here are some tactics that will help you yield a bountiful harvest in the future:

- Become aware of your environment. Learn by emulating successful networkers around you. Identify what they do that appeals to you. Your environment also includes what you read. From now on, look at the news with a "networking" eye, and listen to the news with a "networking" ear. When someone interests you, send a note that compliments that person.

- Be "results oriented" and have a plan. Make networking a part of your daily routine. For example, if you're off to an association meeting, set a goal to make two new contacts and then follow up with them. Following up is the most crucial part of the process. It separates the pros from the amateurs. If you think it's time-consuming to develop a relationship with the new people you meet, you're right. You'll never know in advance which "lead" will turn out to be productive unless you take the time and effort to find out.

- Find an original approach. For example, with my business, I have an easy-to-read e-zine that I email to customers, prospects, and friends. It is also mailed to people I meet at trade shows. Take the initiative and be the one to make the first move. The person who hesitates is lost. Make it brief and to the point.

- Be a joiner and get involved. Sitting on the sidelines won't get you noticed. Have an active life. I recently joined a business club where I can entertain clients and enhance my own network. I immediately wrote a letter to the president of the club, and asked him how I could get involved with some of the committees. He called me back, and the first thing he said was, "I like your direct approach." My networking did not stop with him; I also became friendly with the support people there, remembering them with a note of appreciation. Think about the business organizations in which you can actively participate.

- Perception is reality. People remember what they see and hear from you. Make a good first impression that never stops impressing others. Treat new contacts with special care and importance.

Reintroduce yourself to those individuals who are still getting to know you.

- Have measurable tactics. Every good strategy has specific action steps that can be monitored. For example, each week call three people you haven't spoken to in 90 days. Keep a log of contacts along with the type of follow-up you used. Decide which approaches are working best for you. Although you can scientifically measure results, remember that networking is an art form expressed by you.

This chapter gave you more food for thought in business, life, and making and creating connections. Act on one of these tips right now.

4

Building Relationships

Networks develop when we build relationships with others in our professional and personal life. It starts with liking the other person, learning from them, and establishing trust, all of which takes time, patience and continual nurturing.

Tip 1: Get to Know Your Contacts—Put Their Information into the Information Bank

Here is my list of information to know about your contacts, clients, and prospects as you get to know them. Some items are obvious and some only develop over time as the relationships grow—and they will as you listen, record, and find out new information. Data is key, and we are always looking to expand our relationships with more information.

Business information:

- Company/firm
- Business background/previous work experience
- Address/phone number
- Assistant's name
- Promotions/business opportunities
- Key relationships
- Corporate culture, levels, politics
- "Why do you work with us?"

- How you met
- What business issues are they working on now?
- Who you refer them to and why
- Immediate business/career objectives
- Personality type: Driver, Expressive, Analytical, Amiable
- Did you ask for their advice? Information given?
- How they've handled challenges in the past
- Which competitor they're most concerned about
- How they receive information: online, print, TV/radio
- What contributions are they most proud of?
- Preferred method of communication: email/phone/text/other
- Anniversary of doing business together
- What "motivates" them
- What achievement makes them proud
- Professional associations

Personal information:

- Birthday
- Birth state or country
- Activities in community/charities
- Education: high school, college, fraternity or sorority, degrees
- Military service
- Hobbies/personal interests
- Favorite foods/restaurants
- Vacation interests
- Spouse: name, occupation, and interests
- Children: names, ages, schools, interests

- Pets

- Personal objectives

- Key extended family members

- Special holidays

- Any specific likes and dislikes

- Book genre they enjoy reading

- Collections they may have

- How often they wish to be communicated with

- Idiosyncrasies

- Anything else?

Tip 2: Make Clients for Life

Think about making clients for life starting now. In today's competitive world, you need to be proactive about maintaining and improving relationships with your existing clients. As you do this, in genuine ways, you deepen the ties you have as associates in business *and* as fellow colleagues. Here are some ways to further these relationships (and remember, some of your "clients" can be your internal co-workers or business units within your organization):

- Spend 30 minutes each day talking with two existing clients or friends. Ask them what they want, what they need, and what they like/don't like. Implement the ideas that work for you.

- Invite your "champion clients" to serve on your board of directors. Your clients will add wisdom and will know that you value their judgment.

- Post articles about your clients' achievements in your organization. People love to be acknowledged for their wins.

- Invite clients/customers to test a new product or service before you offer it to the public. Your customers will have insight about trends and what the public wants. This will save you energy and will send the message to your client that they are the first to experience something new.

- Partner with your clients in a marketing effort, workshop, or special event. The more opportunities you have to spend with your clients, the more you will connect on a personal basis.

- Provide value every day. Giveaways and discounts are a great way to retain clients and attract new ones. Offer something unique to show your customers that you are creative and open to new ideas. Make sure it is something they would like.

- Follow the successes of companies that have a reputation for outstanding customer service. By learning from the pros, your business will grow and improve.

- Connect with your clients through common interests. Find out what you share in common with your clients. They will remember you and develop a sense of friendship.

- Your clients are always right even if they're wrong. Thank your customers for both positive and negative comments. Do everything in your power to make them happy.

Keep these tips in mind everyday as you expand your network of clients and contacts.

Tip 3: From Complaint to Opportunity

Sometimes a complaint is an opportunity in disguise. When we take the time to truly listen to our customer vent or tell us what is wrong, there is a window of time where we can turn that into something positive and possibly create a loyal customer:

- Listen to the customer's complaint.

- Take complaints seriously and act fast.

- Empower everyone in your organization to handle complaints.

- Avoid focusing on fixing the blame.

- Let the customer suggest alternatives.

- Minimize the time between a complaint and when it is resolved.

- Trust in the customer's sincerity.

- Empathize with the customer.

Tip 4: People You Need in Your Network

You can learn something from almost everybody you come into contact with in your life, which benefits you both professionally and personally. People you meet may also know others who can help you. An important first step in expanding your network is to identify the people with whom you want to build relationships. As described in Chapter 1, "Networking Is a Mindset," the types of people you need in your network include the following:

- Customers/clients

- Suppliers

- Neighbors

- Like-minded people

- People you meet by chance

- Friends

- Family

- Social media colleagues

Write down the names of people you know in each of these categories who would return your email, text, call, or LinkedIn invitation. Then think of a specific reason why you should contact them. For example, if you know that your neighbor is a real estate agent, tell them about an article you saw concerning trends in property values. The point is to find a meaningful way to connect with people that will benefit them.

Tip 5: It's All About Your Clients

Finding clients and nurturing them is one key ingredient to success. Each of these people can become an advocate to help you grow your business. Satisfied clients, business contacts, friends, and team members can be your best sales and marketing champions because they know and respect you. Here are some ways to earn the trust of your clients, both internal and external, and stay on their radar screens:

- Befriend your clients. Have a meal with them or take them to an event. Develop a relationship with your clients as you would with a friend. They often do become one.

- Provide dazzling service. Credibility is everything. Provide top service and always go the extra mile.

- Place their needs first. Be proactive. Find ways to make their life and work easier and more productive.

- Be their advocate. Make connections for your clients. Help them find new business, a valuable connection, or anything that enhances their life or solves a problem.

- Refrain from keeping score. Do this because you like and respect them. When you show that you are thinking about them and they're always on your radar screen, you'll find yourself on theirs as well.

- Keep giving your clients added value. Increase your services to them. In addition to what you are already doing, send them a new suggestion, idea, strategy, or a tip of the month (or week) that will help grow their business.

Using these strategies, you will earn your clients' trust and respect over time and will see the results in a solid network of contacts. They will become your advocates and talk about you and your business in a positive way. This is a credibility factor that comes from working hard and smart to create powerful connections.

Tip 6: Ways to Sharpen Your Business Edge

Take the time to develop your ideas and action plans to build your competitive edge. I once heard "in the grocery store of life, why would someone pick you off the shelf?". Are you new and improved? We live in a world where every single thing we do is part of our personal brand.

- Pay attention to articles as well as YouTube and TV shows about trends and changes in national and international demographics. This information can be very helpful in finding new business opportunities for you, thus increasing profits and ideas for providing additional value and service for the people who do business with you.

- A marketing plan is only as good as the tracking system you put in place. It will enable you to see where your dollars are being the most beneficial to your business. Track each client or request for additional information. Get in the habit of asking your clients, "How did you hear about us?" Then keep that information in your contact system along with their name, address, and any special requests or preferences they may have.

- It is important to know how a client found you and then to thank that person or source (more business will come from it). You will see patterns begin to emerge that will help you focus your marketing efforts where they are the most effective.

- Joining your local Chamber of Commerce and/or other trade associations will give you more places to network and connect with other business people. You will be able to share experiences and bounce new ideas off of them. At the same time, you can share your experiences and solutions to problems they may be facing. More and more, the business world works best when businesses co-partner and act in a mutually interdependent way. It is all about collaboration.

- You are always marketing your business and yourself. Even if you don't think you are in a "business setting," you are still conveying an impression of yourself and your business. Be helpful and listen to people. Helping people is rewarding all by itself, and you will find that other people notice and will think of your business first when they need the product or service you provide. They'll know you are committed to the community and to helping others because you helped them.

- When advertising, think targeted. Find out how your clients spend their time, what they read, and what they like to do in their free time (besides spend it with family). Then use this information to help you target your marketing efforts so your message will directly reach the people who are interested in your product or service.

- Develop different ways for potential clients to get to know you. Writing articles, doing workshops, and speaking at meetings are great ways to interact with your potential networks. They will get to meet you and experience your style first hand. If you are uncomfortable doing these things, think of ways to start small and build your confidence. Find a way to give a presentation at one of your associations or do a YouTube video on a subject that you have expertise on.

- Be consistent in your communications. What is most important to you? What is the essence of what you provide to your clients that is fulfilling to you? Narrowing your focus and determining what you want to share will help you define your business style. You can then have all of your marketing materials reflect that style. This will attract the best clients for you.

- Help people find "doable" ways to start and then to continue to work with you. Think of ways you can tailor your services to smaller businesses or organizations so they can begin working with you in a limited way and grow into more services or products. Offer different services with different price points. People like to test things out; make sure they feel comfortable and are pleased with the services you provide. Let them experience first-hand the value you provide and realize that they want to continue to do more business with you.

- Define the kinds of client projects or goals you would enjoy working with most. Are there clients in a particular industry or generation or have a personal philosophy that you would like to work with? What about clients who present a greater level of challenge? When you focus on the kinds of clients and projects important to you, you will attract those who are most rewarding for you to work with. You'll be excited by the work you do together and have a great person to refer you to other potential clients with these same qualities. Go where they go, read what they read, and start to integrate yourself.

Tip 7: The First Call Is the Beginning of Many

Follow up with cards, notes, gifts, or get-togethers. Find opportunities to stay on the "memory screens" of your contacts. Focus on tuning into the radio station MMFIAM—"Make Me (the other person) Feel Important About Myself." Stay in touch, learn about them, and make connections that will be helpful in their life. Here are five convenient ways to remain connected to your business contacts:

- **Handwritten notes**—Send a personal note in the form of an "FYI" (For Your Information), "Congratulations," "Nice talking to (or meeting) you," "Thinking of you," or "Thought you would be interested." Because handwritten notes are so rare, the ones you write will make an impression.

- **Holiday cards**—Seasons greetings and special occasion cards let your contacts know you care about what's special to them. Consider the profile and interests of your contact when sending a card. Your recipients will continue to be surprised and happy to hear from you. I use a very cool system that allows me to send real, physical cards and campaigns all through the computer, yet the mail is delivered to your recipient's office or home mailbox. Go to www.appreciationpower.com and send a free card on me to see how it works.

- **Interesting emails**—A creative email with a message tailored to your recipient can also make you stand out. Forward interesting online articles and websites, inspirational quotes, pictures, videos, or a monthly tip. Personalize your emails with a friendly note or signature and keep your contact's needs in mind. Again, social media makes this easy and fun.

- **Your blog, articles, or newsletter**—Send your contacts your own published articles or create one if you have yet to do so. Compile your articles into a blog with tips and techniques that can help advance their business. Write a personal note with each article or newsletter to grow and keep these relationships.

- **Gifts**—Sending a nice gift sets you apart and shows your contacts your appreciation. Whether sending food, flowers, or a book, be sure to consider your recipient's preferences and habits. Send a gift that can be shared with others in the company. Do what works for you and makes your client happy, and remember to keep it professional. And think, "How would I react getting this particular gift?" Think it through—one size does not fit all.

Think of staying in touch as proactive and as a nice way to nurture your network regularly. When the opportunity arises to ask for some advice, you can do it easily because you have built a solid relationship.

Tip 8: A Simple Note Goes a Long Way

Successful networking means an effective follow-up strategy for building up your contacts, connections, and trusted advisors. After any meeting, it is important to connect with your new contacts and follow up with your friends or acquaintances to nurture them. Because timing is of the essence, be sure to follow up quickly, efficiently, and genuinely. It is the key to growing your network and business.

The following are the four "must-dos" after a meeting:

1. **Generate a greeting.** Within 24 hours after a meeting, send a note, email, or call to let your new contacts know how much you appreciated getting to know them. Doing this distinguishes you so that you stand out. I am still amazed how often this is not done.

2. **Present your promise.** When you promised to send materials, call to set up a meeting, or give a referral, keep your word. Following up in a timely manner will establish you as a trustworthy person. Under-promise and over-deliver.

3. **Dial the digits.** Within two weeks after suggesting a get-together, call your new contact and set up a lunch or more formal meeting. Always send a courtesy email, text, or call to confirm the day before. Your sincerity and professionalism will shine through.

4. **Give the gift of thanks.** When a contact provides you with a referral or offers to pass along your information, be sure to thank them and keep them in the loop by letting them know the

developments and results that occur. These simple gestures of appreciation go a long way when building and maintaining your network.

These follow-up acts are purely common courtesy and professionalism. They help build solid relationships for the future, and show respect for others. "Respect" is the key word. Remember, people do business with those whom they know, respect, and like.

Tip 9: Develop Advocates

Who is your advocate? Your clients can be. In business, networking is a necessary skill for finding and developing new clients and retaining those you have. It's also an opportunity to create advocates for your business. These advocates will be your best sales and marketing champions because they know and respect you. Here are some potential advocates you might consider:

- **The satisfied client**—Where else could you find a better advocate? Though you may feel awkward asking for referrals, there are ways to make asking easier. For instance, ask for feedback after you have provided a product or service. Then, if it's positive, suggest you would be "happy to work with anyone else they could recommend."

- **Your team**—Everyone from the new intern up should be aware that they are an ambassador for spreading the work about your company. Smart networkers know to build relationships and alliances with those who are above them organizationally as well as down, sideways, and across. This is a key point. Keep in touch with receptionists, office administrative people, and those in other departments to stay informed of leads they may develop for you. Think how you can be of help to them and what you can learn.

- **Colleagues in business**—In today's specialized world, many of the contacts you make in your industry will refer business to you because you specialize in an area that is needed. Fine tune a 20-second "infomercial" about your services or products that will "stick" with people long after the conversation has concluded (see Tip 10 for more on this).

- **Friends and neighbors**—You work hard at building friendships based on mutual trust and respect. As you find out more about your friends' and neighbors' work, you'll want to help them, and over time they will most likely want to help you if they can. Always put the relationship first when networking with personal connections. Yet, always be aware that opportunities come up in places you may least expect!

Of course, even when you've made advocates, you still need to market yourself directly to prospects and clients. When your advocates open the door for you, you must stay in there and move the project to the next level. The more advocates believe in you, the more convincing they'll be with new clients. Make a list of your advocates and get a plan together to cultivate these relationships starting today!

Tip 10: What Do You Do? Your 20-Second Infomercial

The most commonly asked question at networking events is, "What do you do?" How you respond can be the beginning of a great business relationship. You must be prepared to answer this question in a clear, concise, enthusiastic, and memorable way—all in 20 seconds or less! This statement is called your 20-second infomercial (or "hook" or "grabber"). Here are some questions to help you determine whether your personal introduction is effectively communicating who you are:

- **Does my opening statement make the other person say, "Tell me more?"** Your statement needs to leave your contact eager to find out more about who you are. Offer a brief and exciting description of how you serve or help people.

- **Am I specific or unique enough?** Make yourself stand out. Be sure to paint a word picture in the other person's mind that is easy to visualize.

- **Do I enjoy what I do, and does it show?** Come across as enthusiastic and upbeat. When you're excited about your work or professional interests, you naturally come across as an energetic and passionate person.

- **What benefits and solutions to problems do I provide?** Offer yourself as a problem solver. Always think of how you convey what you do as a benefit to the other person or a solution to a problem.

- **What makes me and my services unique?** Distinguish yourself from the competition. Your grabber has to convey your exclusivity and the service you provide. Your personal introduction statement has to be particularly appealing when meeting someone for the first time. When preparing it, think about how you want to be remembered as well as what will make you stand out and show your uniqueness.

Think of several different introductions, based on each audience, group, and market you serve—the list goes on. Keep coming up with unique and innovative ways to describe "who you are."

Tip 11: Gratitude—and Your Attitude

Always say thank you. Thank you! Thank you! Thank You! You can't say it enough with sincerity.

Take time every day to say thank you to those who have contributed to your continuing success. When you start thanking each person who has made a contribution to your life in some way, you will see the power of this simple, yet amazing part of etiquette.

Showing sincere appreciation to others is so important that I created a technique that I call the "Thank You Chain." For every workshop, keynote address, presentation, or referral, I thank everyone who was involved in securing the opportunity. It is frequent that a project or business comes from a collective effort, and I want to make sure everyone knows that their part of it was deeply appreciated.

Start your own "Thank You Chain" by taking the following steps:

1. Work from the past to present, thinking about the chain of events that led to your current career position or most recent business opportunity.

2. Make a list of the people who helped you, through referrals, endorsements, advice, or in other ways.

3. Call, send a personalized email, or (my favorite) take out a pen and paper and write a handwritten note to thank them for their confidence in you. Report how you are doing and how their assistance positively impacted your success.

4. Each time you receive a new piece of business or advance in your career, keep the people who helped you up to date and thank them again for the part they played.

One quality that makes people charismatic and positive networkers is their diligence in showing appreciation. I have heard it said that you can never say thank you too many times when it is done sincerely. It is good etiquette, and good etiquette is always good business.

Tip 12: Pulling It All Together

You might be getting overwhelmed with all the suggestions in this book. Just stop, choose one or two tips, and think how they work in your life and work. In fact, at the end of the book in the appendix, I have put together a guide for you with 52 tips, and I encourage you to do two of them a week for six months. Master them and then continue to add and modify others that work for you and continue for the next six months.

You can meet people and network anyplace, anytime. Networking is a "nonstop" process; it is just living your life, connecting with people, learning, giving, and making things happen. Many people give up on networking because they think it is only about handing out business cards and asking for referrals. Nothing could be further from the truth. Building the relationships you need to reach your potential is easier than you think, yet it does take work. Look at it as a simple five-step process:

1. **Meet people.** Welcome opportunities to meet new people, and reconnect with those you already know.

2. **Listen and learn.** Everybody likes to talk about themselves. When you listen, you will learn who they are, what is important to them, how you can help them, and how they can help you.

3. **Make connections.** Help people connect with others you know who can help them.

4. **Follow up.** If you promise to do something, keep your promise, and do it in a timely manner. Follow-up is one of the golden keys of authentic networking.

5. **Stay in touch.** After an initial period of contact, if nothing happens, most people will just move on. Here is where a networking system really "works" for successful networkers. Successful networkers find ways to stay in touch and continue to build relationships. Why? Because their goal is to build a network of long-lasting, mutually beneficial relationships, not just to get an immediate "result."

The following example comes from Steven Georgeou of Geocom, whom I met years ago when I spoke for his MBA alumni. His brief story shows why following up, staying in touch, and reaching out to someone are so important in building a relationship.

> "Recently, I read an article on loyalty written by someone at a loyalty systems company. I noticed in his biography that he had gone to my alma mater, the University of Chicago, and contacted him. We met and this eventually led to my speaking engagement at their annual conference for executives working on frequent flyer programs in St. Paul de Vence. Great conference, great contacts."

Tip 13: Do Your Research

Before you attend a meeting, research who is organizing it. Research the speakers, the topics, and the issues relevant to the meeting. Everything is online and easy to find during your research. Much of the information you learn will lead to opportunities for you to start a conversation with others at the meeting. Be prepared with "get to know you" questions to ask individuals beyond information about the organization or event. These can be questions related to the work they do or to family, travel, hobbies, or favorite books or movies.

Tip 14: Set a Goal for Every Event You Attend

Set a goal before you leave the office to meet two new people at any given event. You can certainly meet more; however, your goal is to meet just two new people with whom you will engage in conversation, ask some open-ended questions, and exchange pleasantries. If there is a reason to meet again, send a note, write an email, make a call, send a text, or make a LinkedIn request to set up a follow-up meeting over breakfast or lunch. In any event, send a short "thank you for your time and conversation" note to the two people, even if there is no future meeting. This is just common courtesy and will serve you well as a respected business person.

The key is to set a goal to make a target number of quality connections at every meeting, gathering, or event you attend. It is also a great time to reconnect with those you already know at an event. Although meeting and connecting with new people is an important part of networking, staying in touch and nurturing relationships with those you already know is the true key and relationship-building factor. And be sure to follow up.

Tip 15: Pay Attention and Ask Questions

The following story was submitted to me by my former client and now friend, Paul Brustowicz, about someone he knew in his community:

> "When a regional bank opened a new office in town, bank officers visited my friend Tom and asked him to be on their advisory board. He demurred, not knowing what he could bring to the bank, yet they insisted. He took the advice of an older colleague, bought some of the bank stock, and networked at advisory board meetings.

"Out of the blue, the bank asked Tom for a proposal on an executive compensation program for their officers. Tom reached out to his home office for help and made the proposal. Seven months later, it became a reality when he was ushered into a conference room with the bank president and 25 officers to take applications for the new plan.

"Over the next few years, more opportunities developed, and throughout it all Tom maintained contact with board members and executives. He did the little things: remembering birthdays and anniversaries, arranging for unique gifts appropriate to the client, such as a special pen, a cricket ball, or a collectible hockey puck, recognition at a public event, concert seats, and box seats at a game.

"Tom's networking skills paid off in many ways. He qualified for numerous company awards, lifetime membership in the Million Dollar Round Table, and many accolades.

"At almost 80 years of age, Tom is still in his office daily to review client files, make calls, and check in with his clients. What else could you ask for after 50 years of enjoying what you do daily. And Tom doesn't even think this is 'networking.'"

Tip 16: Low-Cost Networking Tips for Small Business Owners

As small business owners, we make major investments in marketing through websites, trade shows, and collateral materials. To augment these more expensive efforts, here are some low-cost, easy ways to stay in touch with clients. They work, and only take a short amount of time. Commit to several each week, and watch your business grow:

- **Use the 46-cent investment plan.** The post office is alive and well—and even though the price of a stamp goes up, I believe it is worth it to make the impression you leave when you drop a note in the mail. Mail personal handwritten notes to your clients to say thank you for their business every time. It is a pleasant way to show your appreciation, and it keeps your name in front of them. If the stamp price goes up, you can always buy "forever stamps."

- **Eye the news.** Go through all news journals on and offline with a "marketing" eye. Send articles to clients or prospects that would be interesting to them. Attach a note saying, "Thought you might enjoy this." It shows people that you are thinking of them.

- **Call with a tip.** When you have some inside information or any thoughts or suggestions, call a few select clients and share the news. Even leaving a voicemail says to others, "I'm thinking of you and want to keep you informed." It also shows that you care about their businesses and want to help them grow.

- **Seek advice.** Everyone likes to feel needed. When you call a client or prospect and say, "Help me out. I'd like your advice on something," you're giving that person a very high compliment, which will be remembered.

- **Keep the door open.** Even when you lose an order or a bid, take the time to send sincere follow-up notes to let clients know that you appreciate the time and consideration they gave you.

These tips take very little time and yet have a big pay-off.

Networking is a life-long process. Every contact you meet offers you the chance to learn something new. These contacts enrich your life and lead you to relationships that help you achieve your goals.

5

Where to Network—EVERYWHERE

"Appreciate people in the moments we share with them as the arrow of time changes ideas and hearts. People are constantly evolving and have their own life and dreams. They are in your life either for a reason or season and very rarely a lifetime. Live in the moment, and when it does end, that was your time and that was time enough. Be a quiet advocate of a cause by not bringing attention to yourself, but to the cause. More people are willing to help if they feel they are part of bigger picture. Discover where your comfort zone lies; then push yourself slightly beyond it. In due time, you'll discover more of what the world offers. Acknowledge your limitations and work with it."

—Donald Britt of Don411.com Media
"Performing Arts News and Events U"

My friend Don, who wrote these lines, is the ultimate connector. In Sarasota, Florida, he has created a community by bringing together different forms of culture, such as opera, orchestra, theater, and ballet, while including the sciences, business, animal welfare, and social issues. This creates collaborations and friendships to help further the awareness of the arts without cost to any organization. He does this because he truly adores the arts and appreciates the effort, time, and money it takes to entertain the patrons. He wants to make sure the efforts of those who make art happen do not go unnoticed or unappreciated, which he does through coordinating dinner parties and social events of three to 20 people at select restaurants and venues. He has information printouts to keep the group informed with the exchange of information. He makes a point to continually connect people with synergies who have never met but can benefit in knowing each other. This continues to unfold in all forms and directions, and he seems to know something positive about everyone he comes in contact with. Don has been called the "Social Maestro." As he explains, "I view everyone as unique as a music note, and it is up to me to place each note correctly in a measure for the perfect harmony."

Tip 1: Places to Connect

To give you some "food for thought," here are some places where I have made connections (see how you can add to this list):

- **The post office, at the back of the line**—I was waiting in line at the post office when I struck up a conversation with the person in front of me. The conversation turned to my *College Networking* book, which I just happened to be carrying. I always carry my books—they are my biggest business cards. Whatever your "prop" is, carry it with you at all times. It turned out my fellow post office customer worked with a small manufacturing company that was looking for a consultant to help with a new software system. I knew someone perfect. We exchanged cards, I followed up, and we are building a rapport and relationship.

- **The nail salon**—I was having my nails done one day when I heard another customer chatting about holiday plans. Starting a conversation while our nails dried, I found out the woman was looking for speakers to talk to members of her company as part of their training. I left the salon with freshly polished nails and two business leads.

- **The coffee shop**—I was sitting in a coffee shop talking with a friend about his advertising business. Noticing that a man at the next table was listening, I introduced myself and asked if he was in advertising as well. He said he was but was currently looking for a job. I introduced the two men and later heard that the man at the next table had been granted an interview at my friend's business.

These common themes are why I say, "You never know." Many of the people you meet in everyday life could be a potential networking contact. I have also gathered solid business contacts in the following places:

- On an airplane
- At the dentist's office
- In line for movie tickets
- At the grocery store

The point is to be constantly aware of opportunities to meet new people, because you never know who will turn out to be a great networking contact. As I've said before, always be prepared with your conversation starter. Don't ask for something; offer something, and then follow up.

Good networking consists of practicing good communication skills on a consistent basis and being ready to use those skills in any situation. The most important thing is to follow up; otherwise, a casual conversation will never lead to a business relationship.

Tip 2: Practice Your Networking Skills

Often we learn this lesson after we've been putting our networking strategy to work consistently. Answer the following questions today, next week, and in three months to analyze your "formal" networking progress as you go along:

- What are my personal goals and objectives specific to networking?
- What are some of the barriers that I need to break through?
- How could I be more effective networking with my existing clients, and how will I do this?
- How do I effectively "work the room" at an event, whether I am introverted or extroverted?
- How do I make a memorable impact when meeting someone?
- How do I strengthen my 20-second "sound bite"?
- How do I effectively follow up?

Tip 3: Join the Best Organizations for You and Use the 2-2-2 Strategy

If you have been in your business for a while, you probably know about all the various networking groups available. The question is, how do you choose which one will work for you? Choosing what group you join will determine the effectiveness of your time and money. I recommend a 2-2-2 strategy to decide which organizations and clubs to join. Before you decide to join a group, take these important steps:

1. **Attend two meetings.** This will help you in several ways:

    - You will experience the organization or group first hand.

    - You will see whether the organization will meet your particular needs.

    - You will meet people involved in the organization.

    - You can access a schedule of events and find out their long-term goals.

2. **Meet two people and exchange business cards.** This is an important step in understanding the organization for several reasons:

    - You can ask specific questions about the organization, such as who regularly attends, whether the meetings you attended are typical, and how you can benefit from the group.

    - These two contacts can introduce you to other members.

    - You can find out what kinds of people participate in the group.

3. **Arrange two follow-up meetings for breakfast, lunch, or coffee.** This step is great for its long-term benefits:

    - If you join, these two relationships can multiply into many relationships within the group.

    - Regardless of whether you join or not, you now have two new contacts!

By following this easy 2-2-2 plan, you will find the organizations that best meet your needs. Join and become active in these organizations.

If you choose your organizations carefully, you can use them to make important contacts, grow your business, and expand your network.

Tip 4: The Opposite of Networking Is Not Working

Write this quote down and put it on your computer monitor. Every time you meet someone, you have the opportunity to learn from them or to be a resource to them. It is all about giving first. I like to live by this quote that I made up. Look at it each morning and start the day with a goal in mind of how to put it into practice.

Here is an example: I got a call one morning from Eric, who is someone I had worked with several years before as a participant in a workshop. He remembered me and had now moved into a new position. Turns out he was also looking for a new apartment, and I had just spoken to a friend in the business who was describing a place that almost seemed perfect for him. I connected the two. Several months later, he moved, though not to the first apartment but to another my contact showed him. He then introduced her to three other friends who have all become her clients. I was thrilled—all because I think with a networking mindset.

You might be wondering, did it come back? Remember not to keep score, because things do come back down the road. Eric did in fact have me work with his new company and then introduced me to two other friends, and I have worked for them as well.

So, yes, your network will expand and grow, just as you want it to. However, you must give and be willing to give and let the relationship grow first.

Tip 5: Start a Conversation Today

Approach someone, and do not wait for them to approach you. The key to creating connections is conversation. The secret of conversation is to ask open-ended high-gain questions, such as "What kind of work do you do?" The quality of the information you receive depends on the quality of your questions. When you have a conversation, it may lead to a business relationship. A relationship could lead to new business.

A business relationship when nurtured can and will lead to long-term continued success.

You have to meet someone new in order to welcome and create these opportunities. If nothing else, you will hone your presentation skills—and that is always a major plus.

Tip 6: The Plain Truth About Networking

One of the golden rules of business has long been, "It's not what you know, but who you know."

Although this little piece of advice has significant implications for all of us, it begs the more important question: "Who don't I know, and what and who do they know that I should know?" Of course, the logical follow-up is, "Where and how do I get to know them?"

You can't always leave your home or office with the sole intent that you are going to run into someone and create a network opportunity. Staring at name tags is more likely to create a sore neck than it is an important business or social connection. That said, you should also be prepared to network when an unexpected opportunity arises. Know your own elevator speech. Always try to smile, and always be aware of what is going on around you.

The following story comes from the late Bruce Dorskind concerning an unexpected networking opportunity:

> "One of my most successful connections occurred under the most unusual circumstances, and it is worth sharing because we turned an innocent question into an important opportunity and eventually into a long-term relationship.
>
> "Back in 1980—long before I even knew what networking was—one of my great passions in life was collecting rare old baseball cards. Back then, baseball card collecting was still an under-the-radar hobby and it was difficult to communicate with other collectors except at shows—and most of those were limited to one's local area. For me personally, there was a great deal to learn and very few people to learn from. One of the most knowledgeable

people in the world was a British collector named Sir Edward Wharton Tigar.

"Well, as fate would have it, I was doing some research in the Print Room of the Metropolitan Museum of Art and looking at some rare cards. Unexpectedly, someone asked to borrow some yellow paper and my pencil. The accent was distinguished and unmistakably British. As I turned to my new colleague, I stated, 'You have an English accent. By chance do you know that distinguished British card collector, Sir Edward Wharton Tigar?'

"To my astonishment, he replied, 'It is I.' And thus began a seven-year friendship (until his passing). A wonderful interchange of knowledge, a few card trades, and some lovely social evenings. As it turns out, Sir Edward was a world-class thinker and one of the most interesting people I ever met (certainly the most interesting I ever met by accident)."

Tip 7: Reconnect with Contacts You Already Know

Find ways to nurture relationships. Here are a few hints. I know I'm repeating myself, yet these are vital to your networking success:

- **Listen and learn.** Everyone likes to talk about themselves. When you listen, you will learn who they are, what is important to them, how you can help them, and how they can help you.

- **Make connections.** Help people connect with others you know who can help them.

- **Follow up.** When you promise to do something, keep your promise and do it in a timely fashion.

- **Stay in touch.** After an initial period of follow-ups, even if no business has resulted from those initial contacts, find ways to stay in touch. This way, you'll continue to build a network of long-lasting, mutually beneficial relationships.

Tip 8: Keep Contacts on Your Radar Screen

Whether you're at work, at the health club, at the store, on a trip, or in your community, keep people on your radar. I buy clients and friends gifts when I see something they would like (refer back to my contact information list at the beginning of Chapter 4, "Building Relation-ships"). One of my friends loves giraffes. Knowing this, I've been able to find the most unusual "giraffe gifts" for her. I seem to find things everywhere. Think about your own clients and friends. It's like red cars. You may never see them or notice them, until you decide to buy one and then they seem to be *everywhere*!

Tip 9: Do It Now—Every Day—Instead of Waiting for Holidays

Every day is a holiday when you remember someone. When I was in a Los Angeles hotel gift shop, I found a book of New York poems for my friend Bill (I know, New York poems in LA?), as well as two leather notebooks for friends (one friend is writing his life stories and the other loves keeping a journal). I also found an unusual candle for another client who uses candles to decorate her office. Be alert and think as you find something along your daily path, "Who might like and enjoy this?". Every day can be a holiday.

Tip 10: The Business "Setting" (or Elevator Awareness)

Always be ready and able to pull out the answers to the following ques-tions whenever you meet a new contact:

- At a conference, meeting, convention, or a client call: What is your business pitch?

- Do you have your networking toolkits at all times? Are you ready to hand out business cards and/or record information about new contacts or update previous contacts?

Remember, take the big step and approach someone new. Get out of your comfort zone. Networking is a leadership skill you'll develop as you practice your communication skills. Be the leader and form your own group; serve on your local professional organization's board; get involved with your community; mentor others as they move up in their careers; teach others in organizational courses or workshops; volunteer to make a speech on a subject pertinent to your group; write and publish articles; create your own website as a marketing tool.

Recognize that good relationships require nurturing, not "work." Also, genuine results cannot be forced when you meet new people. They develop over time as you get to know and appreciate each other.

Tip 11: Networking Takes Time and Patience

When you network, you must learn to respect others' timetables. Of course, sometimes new contacts do not respond in a timely fashion. They may be busy with their own deadlines and have a lot of responsibilities, and therefore cannot immediately respond to you. So, how can you move the networking process forward without "pushing" too hard?

Ask your contact their preferred method of communication when you reach out. Some people prefer that everything be done in writing, whereas others would rather receive a quick follow-up phone call or email alerting them to new opportunities that can benefit them. Others may ask for a text or for you to connect with them via social media. It is their preference and choice. It will show that you listened to them.

Check on new contacts regularly. In my experience, the long-term follow-up is very important. Mark your calendar for the next significant date on your contacts' calendar.

Develop a networking action plan. New contacts will not develop into anything important without long-term nurturing. Keep a list of all contacts readily available. Using that list, develop a plan that is appropriate for each of your contacts. Some may be reached through one general method, such as a newsletter; however, most will require unique treatment. For instance, an effective follow-up for one contact may be as simple as seeking them out at an upcoming business function, whereas another contact might appreciate a note with helpful information on a subject you've discussed previously.

Once you discover what is effective, build on what works and develop the skills you need, such as writing and speaking, to make meaningful connections with those people.

Tip 12: Making Networking Practical

There are two main areas of focus when using positive networking tactics: how contacts are identified and appropriate follow-up.

Identifying Potential Contacts

Once you understand how to approach networking from a positive standpoint, you can use techniques that are specific for each of the following categories of contacts:

- **Satisfied customers.** What better referral? They can be the best advocates because they know what you have to offer. You can ask them to introduce you to other people. Most importantly, thank them with a personal note or phone call.

- **Friends.** You work hard at building your friendships, including establishing mutual trust. You can find out about your friends' work and help them. Then, when the time is right, you can ask them for a referral.

- **Neighbors.** Make the effort to strike up conversations with people in your building or neighborhood. You'll often find out that you have common interests with them.

- **Happy, helpful people.** These are the people all of us meet by chance or connect with in unexpected ways. You might meet them on a plane, train, or waiting in line at the movies. Life has a funny way of connecting us when we least expect it. We just have to be ready for the opportunity.

Follow-Up Tactics

Effective networking is based on simple tactics. Here are my Seven Rules of Networking to live by:

1. **Smile.** A smile is a universal welcome sign. The people we meet for the first time will appreciate our warmth.

2. **Look the person in the eye.** It's a compliment to look at someone. It's a way to connect with someone new in the shortest time possible.

3. **Listen.** One of the greatest compliments we can give other people is to let them know that we are listening to them. Remember, when we are networking with new contacts, it's like reading the paper. Let people tell their stories so we can discover the "news we can use."

4. **Pay attention to body language.** First impressions are lasting ones. Monitor expressions. Sometimes, we need to loosen up because meeting new people can make us tense.

5. **Avoid being pushy.** Be careful of coming on too strong. Even if you just lost your job, avoid having new people think you are desperate.

6. **Give genuine compliments.** Yes, even with new contacts, a compliment might be appropriate. When we listen to people carefully, often they will mention something that they are proud of. We need to think for a moment and find a way to sincerely acknowledge others' achievements.

7. **Business cards are golden.** Ask for people's cards, yet only offer yours when requested. When we do get their cards, we should treat them as fine treasures and give them the most respect.

Networking is a process, one that can create business connections to last a lifetime. As someone who works in sales, you are constantly developing, building, and cultivating relationships that can give you results beyond your expectations.

Tip 13: Power of Three Personal Communications in Networking

The "Power of Three" consists of writing a follow-up note to three contacts a day. The United States Postal Service tells us that only 4 percent of the mail is personalized. Therefore, sending notes will put you ahead of 96 percent of the population. Here are some good examples where personal notes work particularly well:

- **"I heard something good about you."** If you hear about someone's personal achievement or if you read something positive about their company, that provides a good opportunity to send a note.

- **Give away information.** For example, if you participate in a Chamber of Commerce, invite a contact to join you as your guest for a special program by sending a note with a copy of the event.

- **Gone, yet not forgotten.** Even if your contacts have clearly stated that they are not interested right now in communicating with you, a follow-up note offering some valuable information is a good way to keep current and potential customers aware of you and your company.

If you absolutely are not a note writer, send three additional emails or texts or make three phones calls to do your own Power of Three.

Tip 14: Developing Your 20-Second Infomercial

In Chapter 2, "Positioning Yourself and Creating Your Brand," we explored the importance of a personal brand statement (PBS) and why it is important when you meet new people, to let them know quickly and clearly who you are and what you are. You need to do this in a way that is concise, enthusiastic, and memorable. Sometimes a PBS is too long. You may only have time for a 20-second "infomercial" about yourself that keeps people interested using the following S.T.R.A.T.E.G.Y.:

S   Make your infomercial **short** and **succinct**.

T   **Think** of it in advance.

R   **Remember** the **results** you want to achieve.

A   Be **articulate** in your message.

T   **Time** is of the essence—20 seconds or less is optimal.

E   Speak with **enthusiasm** and **energy**.

G   Set a **goal** to attain.

Y   Focus on the "**you**," meaning the person you're speaking to.

If you carefully plan how you introduce yourself, you will start dynamic conversations that lead to more information about your new contact and ways you can keep meeting. Always make the person you are speaking with curious and interested. Tell them something that will stay in their mind when they think of you. The bottom line is to introduce yourself in a way that will make people want to know you better. Developing those relationships is the heart of networking.

6

Networking Etiquette

Etiquette is no more than showing respect for other people's feelings and sensitivities. Learning to be an effective networker involves the same kind of respect for the people you meet. It takes networking etiquette to turn chance acquaintances into long-term friends and business associates. It's about building trust; displaying respect, good manners, and common courtesy are key.

Tip 1: The Ten Rules of Business Etiquette

Here are my rules of business etiquette. These ten rules will make networking at events and meetings a positive experience:

1. **It's better to arrive early than late.** An early arrival shows enthusiasm for the event and respect for other people's time. It also affords you the opportunity to meet more people.

2. **Position your name tag so people can easily see it.** Place your name tag on your right-hand lapel. When meeting contacts, this will allow people to see your name better as they shake your right hand.

3. **Exchange business cards with ease and grace.** Fresh, neat business cards are a must. Place them in a pocket where they are easily accessible and be sure to keep yours separate from the cards you receive.

4. **Silently communicate your interest.** Make eye contact and keep it. It is noticeable when your eyes are wandering around the room searching for a "better" contact. Looking someone in the eye shows respect and interest.

5. **Extend a confident greeting.** Make your handshake firm, professional, and genuine. Bone crusher and jellyfish handshakes come across as intimidating and insecure, respectively. A sincere greeting will make a lasting impression.

6. **Avoid invading personal space.** Be aware of your contact's personal space. Moving in too close while conversing makes people uncomfortable. Most people consider anything closer than 18 inches too close and will back away from you. This varies in other countries, so do a little body-language homework before you travel.

7. **Gracefully join conversations.** Be sure to ask for permission to join a conversation in progress. Simply say, "This looks like a fun group, may I join in?" or "How do you all know each other?" You can tailor your request to fit your personality. People enjoy having you connect with them when you are courteous.

8. **Avoid the awkwardness of chewing or handling food while you converse.** Although many events and meetings offer refreshments, refrain from eating and carrying on a conversation at the same time. It takes a lot of experience to balance a plate and eat while conversing. I don't recommend it.

9. **Nonalcoholic networking is the best.** A nonalcoholic drink without ice is the easiest to handle. Why no ice? Frigid handshakes are unpleasant. Why nonalcoholic? You'll pay better attention.

10. **Politely exit conversations.** Your objective at networking events should be to develop several connections. Talking with someone, learning about them and how to follow-up, exchanging business cards, and moving on is an accepted practice. When exiting a conversation, politely express pleasure at having met the individual and the hope that you will meet again. Develop your strategy and follow up.

Successful business relationships, just like successful personal relationships, rely on common courtesy. Following these simple rules of etiquette will create a more relaxing opportunity for networking and your aptitude to be well received at events and meetings.

Tip 2: How to Exit with Grace

Networking events are full of professionals to whom you can be of service or who can help you. In these situations, be sure to consider other people's time because they may also have others to meet during an event. Set your own goals to meet people, but learn to exit gracefully when you've finished your conversation. Here are some polite exit lines that allow you to leave without offense:

- "It was great meeting you, and I hope we can continue our conversation sometime over lunch or coffee."

- "Thanks for sharing the information about your new project. It sounds exciting. Best of continued success."

- "Let me introduce you to [name of another nearby colleague]. He may be a good person to discuss some of the opportunities you have."

- "I'm so glad we met. Lots of good luck, and if I hear of anything that might be a fit for you, I'll definitely be in touch."

- "I enjoyed hearing about your company and look forward to seeing you again."

- "My time has already been well spent having met you. Thank you."

Before starting your exit, if you would like to follow up or your new contact gave you a piece of advice, always ask for their contact information. Remember to follow up with at least a short note and perhaps an email or call to arrange a future meeting. Over time, you'll begin to build rapport and learn about each other, as you establish a solid relationship. Also, realize that at events, people want to talk with others, so never monopolize anyone too long (for me, seven to ten minutes is just right).

Tip 3: A Simple Note Goes a Long Way

After any meeting, it is important to connect with your new contacts and follow up with your friends or acquaintances to nurture them. Because timing is of the essence, be sure to follow up quickly, efficiently, and genuinely. It is the key to growing your network and business by building your contacts, connections, and trusted advisors. The following are the four "must-dos" after a meeting:

1. **Generate a greeting.** Within 24 hours after a meeting, send a note or email or place a call to let your new contacts know how much you appreciated getting to know them. Doing this distinguishes you and makes you stand out.

2. **Present your promise.** When you promised to send materials, call to set up a meeting or give a referral. Keep your word. Following up with the materials you promised in a timely manner will establish you as a trustworthy person. As I've said before, under-promise and over-deliver.

3. **Call or email.** Within two weeks after suggesting a get-together, call your new contact and set up lunch or a more formal meeting. Always send a courtesy email or call to confirm the day before. Your sincerity and professionalism will shine through.

4. **Give the gift of thanks.** When a contact provides you with a referral or offers to pass your information along, be sure to say thank you and keep that person in the loop by letting them know the developments and results that occur. These simple gestures of appreciation go a long way when building your network.

Thanking contacts for their time and their attention is an important way to show them your respect. Offering them something tangible such as a referral, information, or a simple meal shows you care. Remember, people do business with those whom they know, respect, and (often) like.

Tip 4: The Power of the Personal Note

I feel so strongly about the power of the personal note, I want to emphasize it further in this tip. The art of writing personal notes is sadly disappearing. A personal note is one of the best ways to connect or reconnect with others.

Just as a reminder, here are seven reasons to send a thank-you note:

1. For time and consideration.

2. For a compliment you received.

3. For a piece of advice given.

4. For business.

5. For a referral.

6. For a gift.

7. For help on a project.

Thank-You Notes

Thank-you notes are one of the least expensive and most effective networking tools. Always carry notes and stamps with you. Then, whenever you have some "found time"—in an airport, on a train, waiting at a doctor's office, or watching TV—you can dash off a note, address it, and pop it in the mail.

FYI Notes

Don't forget those "FYI notes" that show you have your contact's best interests in mind and help you keep in touch at any time. You can send many things, such as clippings and articles, to a person. This lets them know several things:

- You were thinking of them when you read it.

- You know what they are interested in.

- You care about their business.

Notes of Congratulations

Congratulations are a perfect opportunity to let someone know you are cheering them on. You can give these out on many occasions:

- Promotions

- An award or honor

- An anniversary

Nice Talking to (or Meeting) You Notes

These thoughtful notes help a person to remember you fondly. You can send these out after several events:

- A meeting

- A chance encounter

- A phone conversation

Tip 5: The Power of Email

Email is not quite as personal as a handwritten note, yet it is a powerful way to keep in touch with your network regularly and our most efficient form of business communication. Here are a few guiding principles for making your emails count:

- Keep your e-mails brief and focused.

- Use meaningful subject lines.

- Use a format: purpose, body, and action.

- If you need to send a long document, sent it as an attachment.

- Always reread your message before you hit Send. Make sure your tone is what you want it to be. Avoid anything that could be construed as sarcasm or innuendo.

- Answer all emails within 24 hours. If you are going to be away from your computer, use the "away from my desk until..." message available in most email programs.

Tip 6: Who Introduces Who

In today's business world, making proper introductions is often essential to finding new contacts. Whether in person, through email, or over the phone, polite professional conduct is essential to keeping and growing your network. Here are Nierenberg's Rules of Order:

1. Defer to position and age. Gender is not a factor. An introduction is normally made in the following order—the younger, less senior, executive or person to the older:

   - Introduce younger to older.

   - Introduce your company peer to a peer in another company.

   - Introduce a junior to a senior executive.

   - Introduce a fellow executive to a client.

   - Introduce a personal contact to a business contact.

2. When making introductions, give a brief statement about each person's interest or profession, or better yet, something the two might have in common. This is polite and gets the conversation going.

3. Avoid using nicknames unless it is the person's business name. Use full names and titles such as "Dr." to show respect when you know they always use it.

4. Speak slowly and clearly so each name can be heard.

Tip 7: Good Manners at Non-Networking Events

Networking can happen everywhere. Whether in an elevator, at a sporting event, or waiting in line, opportunities can pop up to help you connect with others. You are eager to meet people who may become your friends and business associates—anyplace, anytime.

However, you also know that networking inappropriately can be destructive to possible relationships. It is important to be considerate of the person to whom you are talking as well as to those around you. Here are a few ways to avoid embarrassment for yourself and your potential contact:

- Recognize where you are and what you are there for. For example, at a funeral, respect and consideration for the bereaved are far more important than meeting acquaintances.

- Be prepared to graciously suggest that you talk about business at a more appropriate time and place. You could say, "This is not a good time to discuss business, so may I give you a call on [date] so we can discuss this further (or so we can consider some options, or so I can help you out)?"

- Ask permission before exchanging business cards, and do so discreetly.

- Remember that some establishments, such as private clubs, simply do not allow the conducting of business. Be aware of this and follow the prescribed behavior.

Successful networkers care about the person they are speaking with as well as those around them. Showing respect is one of the best ways to make and keep contacts. Network whenever and wherever you can, just do so with discretion so that you will avoid embarrassment or giving offense.

Tip 8: Shy Polite People, You Can Network, Too

I have a confession to make. I am an introvert. If you are, too, that's fine—in many ways, we have an advantage over our more assertive colleagues.

You may feel that, despite all your knowledge of networking, you are too shy to network successfully. The idea that networking is only for people with outgoing personalities is really false. Introverts have strengths that they can use with strategies that blend well with their personalities. Here are some real advantages that introverts have for networking:

- Introverts are usually great listeners. They would rather let another person do the talking, and that shows respect toward their colleague.

- They remember details about their contacts, which others might miss. Because they are listening, they can take in more information about their contact.

- They focus on the person they are talking to, making that person feel significant.

- They build sound relationships and care for them because they are often helpful individuals who watch out for others.

- They find the right time to speak—never interrupting or asserting their opinions.

- They are helpful, which often makes others want to be helpful in return.

- They network very well in situations where they can use their skill to help others.

I've found that introverts are almost always passionate about a certain aspect of their business, industry, or product. They speak naturally with enthusiasm and conviction about the things that matter to them. Often, they've learned to overcome their shyness by discussing something they are passionate about. They become extremely effective when they have focus and a genuine reason to make a contact.

By building upon your strengths, fellow introverts, you will become effective networkers. Because you already listen well, help others when you can, and speak well when you are passionate about something, you have the skills to build and nurture strong relationships, which are the keys to great networking.

Tip 9: The Courtesy and Cultivation of Listening Skills

Listening politely shows respect, and is an essential part of making a real connection with people. If you don't listen carefully to what they have to tell you, how can you help them and learn how they can help you?

Rate yourself on a scale of 1 to 5 on these essential active listening skills. Give yourself a 5 if "I always do this with ease and confidence," and 1 if "I rarely do this and feel awkward when I do."

1. I make eye contact. I always look the other person in the eye during our conversation and focus my full attention on them. If it's difficult for me to continue eye contact, I look at the person's "third eye," a spot just above the bridge of the nose between the eyes, realizing that we can only look at one eye at a time anyway.

2. I ask questions for clarification. If I don't understand, I ask the other person to explain so that I can understand better.

3. I show concern by acknowledging feelings. I also listen with my eyes. I use positive body language by nodding and smiling when appropriate.

4. I try to understand the speaker's point of view before giving mine. I recognize that the other person is far more interested in stating their point of view than in hearing mine.

5. I am poised and emotionally controlled. I hold back from jumping to conclusions or interrupting with what I want to say when the other person is speaking.

6. I react nonverbally with a smile or a nod. I know this shows my interest and allows the person to continue without interruption.

7. I pay close attention and do not let my mind wander. I am careful not to allow my mind to take a mental excursion.

8. I avoid interrupting. I always let the other person finish.

9. I avoid changing the subject without warning. Changing the subject abruptly relays that you are not listening and only want to talk about whatever is on your mind.

How did you do?

- If you scored 35–45, you're an **exceptional listener!**

- If you scored 25–34, you're a **very good listener.**

- If you scored 20–24, you're an **average listener.**

- If you scored 15–19, keep working, you'll improve (and maybe should get those Q-Tips out!).

Take a good look at the areas where your rating could improve. Start to work on these while continuing to practice the skills you've already mastered. Take the test again in two weeks. Watch how your ratings increase when you commit to improving your listening skills!

Tip 10: Networking Through Thoughtful Creativity, Persistence, and Respect

Previously we've discussed the importance of personal notes and personal time for nurturing contacts and developing stronger relationships. It's quite easy to write notes, but not so easy to create face-to-face time with people.

Remember my F.A.C.E. tips?

F   Make it **fun** and **friendly**. **Find** unique things to do and places to meet.

A   **Adapt** to each other's timetable and surroundings.

C   **Connect** and find **common** interests.

E   Know when to **exit**. Be respectful of other people's time.

Here are some creative, pleasant ways to meet with your contacts in a cordial sociable way. Extend an invitation to

- meet for coffee, tea, or cappuccino (instead of the traditional breakfast, lunch, or dinner).
- play a fun game of golf, tennis, or bridge.
- go for an invigorating walk, spa treatment, or health club exercise date.
- meet at a museum, art gallery, or store.
- attend an industry event, cocktail party, or trade show.
- join up for a play, concert, or sporting event.
- share a cab to a meeting or meet at the sky club at the airport.

Be creative. Everyone is busy and "business focused," and appreciates new and unique suggestions to relax and learn more about a thoughtful colleague.

Tip 11: Networking Is Not Bad Manners

Having a networking mindset is just the opposite. It is utilizing great manners, both meeting and connecting with new people and deepening the relationship with those you know. The key is being prepared, and this tip will do just that for you. Adapt and modify as you see fit.

1. Give yourself permission to network. Networking is as much nurturing as it is going out to meet people. Changing your attitude to a positive one is the first step to networking success. Realize that "networking" is a state of mind and that it is pure people skills, courtesy, and developing connections.

   As you leave for work every day, give yourself a mental pep talk about connecting and reconnecting with people and setting a goal for yourself each week. Doing simple things such as saying hello to someone you don't know well or sending an email to a colleague in another department can be the first steps to networking success in your business.

2. Prepare yourself by making a list of "opening lines" to use when meeting someone new. Use open-ended questions that require more than a one-word answer, or at least follow up with an open-ended question such as "What brings you to this event?" or "What industry or side of the business are you in?" Practice some opening lines with friends and colleagues so you will be prepared when you go to events. Engage the other person by moving attention from yourself to the other person. Niceness is still key. A warm and approachable smile is always a great icebreaker and the start to your opening lines.

3. Have your 20-second infomercial about yourself ready and practice it until it becomes spontaneous and natural. Ask yourself, "How do I want to be remembered? What is the headline that will grab someone's attention and what is the actual benefit statement when I say what I do?" It is not about a title, such as "I'm the vice president of [fill in the blank]." It's really all the same! More important is *what* you do, so that someone says, "Tell me more." Tell your story well to avoid what I call the "So what?" factor.

4. Use the Internet to establish some relationships with those in your field, specifically for those with an introverted style. Online acquaintances can become an important part of your network. Plan to meet them at professional conferences and trade shows.

5. Do your research before attending an event. Learn the basics about the organization and the people likely to be there. This kind of preliminary research will give you the knowledge you need to focus your conversation on the goals and accomplishments of the people you meet and earn their interest in you. Here is a quick checklist of questions to answer before you go:

   - Who is being honored or speaking?

   - Who will be there?

   - Who do you already know who will be there?

   - What can you learn about them in advance?

6. Set a goal for yourself to meet and connect with at least three people, and develop your list of get-to-know-you questions to help you meet this goal. These should go deeper than opening-line questions, and, as I've said, they help you to get to know the interests of the people you meet. Rapport develops as you start asking and gently probing (never "grilling" or "drilling") and respond to what you learn about the other person and perhaps relate those interests to what you do and how you do it.

Tip 12: Polite Get-to-Know-You Questions

Here are some examples of the kinds of open-ended, cordial questions that invite contacts to converse with you:

- If you could do any kind of work, what would it be, and what makes you say that?

- What do you do when you're not at work (family, hobbies, or special interests)?

- How did you get involved in this industry or group?

- What books or movies or plays have you seen recently?

- What do you like the most about your work and why?

- When you work with _____ (lawyers, bankers, consultants, and so on), what do you look for that makes your job and life easier?

Tip 13: Nurturing, More Long-Range Questions

These are my all-time favorite questions. They give me a reason to follow up and stay in touch, whether it will be in the short term or for a long-range goal:

- How do I know when I'm speaking to a potential client or person you would like to meet (or find a job opportunity you're interested in)?

- What is your preferred method of communication for staying in touch?

It is only after I have asked, listened to, and understood their responses to these questions that I can bring the conversation back to something about me. For example, suppose someone says, "We're looking for consultants who really customize their work to our company and stay on the project from beginning to end." In this case, I might reply, "I totally agree with you, because when I recently worked with XYZ company, the leading reason I got the project was for customization, delivery, and follow-through." Then I could offer a short example of each.

The whole goal is to get people to open up so that they are talking about a subject dear to them, and then you can develop cooperation and rapport. It is only by understanding people's needs that you can demonstrate sincere interest by basing your responses on them.

Tip 14: To Keep the Conversation Going— Keep a Journal of "Small Talk" Topics

Inform yourself about what is happening in the world, and keep a journal of such things as current events, industry topics, books and movies, community topics, sports, celebrities, other items that engage people in the world around us. Start your notebook and let it grow.

Here's another hint: If the conversation has strayed from topics you feel comfortable discussing or topics you want to return to, use a "bridge" phrase such as "That reminds me of..." and then link it back to the topic you had started.

Tip 15: Give Sincere Compliments

Make a goal to look for positive attributes in the people you meet and give five compliments a day. When you look for them, you will find them—but then you must take action. In fact, you should begin every new conversation with a compliment. It is a wonderful way to start when you may be at a loss to break the ice. Everyone likes to hear a compliment when it is sincere.

Tip 16: Telephone Etiquette

In today's business world, few things are as important as communicating your message in a professional manner. The most important person is the one you are talking with. Give your full attention. The telephone also is one important tool used to find, grow, and keep business relationships. The rules of etiquette apply to telephone calls as well. Respect for your contacts' time and courteous listening skills are key. If you are uncomfortable on the telephone, write yourself a simple script and practice until it comes naturally. It is like having your "notes at the podium"—only the other person can't see them! To keep your calls from going too long, have a plan of action laid out for what you want to accomplish by each telephone call.

Here are some other quick telephone tips:

- Return all phone calls within 48 hours.

- When making a call, ask if it is a good time to talk. If not, schedule a more convenient time.

- State the purpose of your call and indicate you would like a few minutes of their time. Do not take any longer.

- When leaving a message, state your name, purpose, and action needed, clearly and succinctly. And, most importantly, when leaving your phone number, speak slowly.

- When calling a contact referral, state your name and who referred you. For example, "Hello [name], my name is Andrea Nierenberg. [So and so] suggested I give you a call about...."

- Avoid multitasking while on the phone. People can hear you typing on your computer or shuffling papers. This shows you are not focused on them. Remember that to do two things at once is to do neither.

Tip 17: Meal Manners

Doing business at a lunch or dinner requires a set of etiquette rules. Here are a few important ones for meals with just you and your contact:

- When ordering, allow your guests to go first and select your entrée accordingly.

- The host directs the server first to the guests and then the host orders last.

- Leave your smartphone in your bag, and on vibrate. If you must accept an essential call, alert your host or guests when you sit down. When the call comes in, excuse yourself, and keep the conversation brief.

- As the host, you should offer the option of dessert, even if you don't want it yourself.

- Keep the dinner napkin on your lap until you rise to leave the restaurant. If you leave the table, put the napkin on your chair until you return.

- Not sure which water glass or salad plate to use? Remember liquids on the right, solids on the left. If your neighbor forgets and takes yours, just ignore it.

- If you are not sure which utensil to use first, working from the outside in is the safest bet.

- When you are finished, place your knife and fork in a parallel position across the center of your plate. This signals for the waiter to clear your place. However, even if you are still hungry, stop eating when everyone else is finished. If you are a fast eater, slow your pace to match others.

- Hold off talking about business until after the main course is removed. This allows time for getting acquainted. The servers will also be out of the way. You have time to discuss over coffee. If this is a breakfast meeting, you can start the business discussion after the orders are placed.

- It is perfectly acceptable to take notes at a business dinner or networking event; just ask first out of courtesy. Then use a small notepad, not an SUV-sized day planner.

- Remember, always carry a mini etiquette survival kit with you: a notepad, pens, business cards, Kleenex, hand sanitizer, comb, and breath mints.

Meeting contacts at a larger business function involves a few more general etiquette rules:

- First introduce yourself to the person seated to your right and left. Then introduce yourself to the rest of the table. As others join your table, introduce yourself and others to them.

- Wait for those at the head table to begin eating. Or, if you're at a private meal, wait for the host or hostess to begin. If you are the host or hostess, you must begin first.

Tip 18: Other Etiquette "Don'ts" to Remember

Often things we wish people didn't notice about us are the first things they remember.

That is why you want to be sure with your networking etiquette that you steer clear of any of the following:

- Getting too personal
- Complaining

- Finishing other's sentences
- Interrupting the other person
- Using profanity or inappropriate jokes
- Dressing inappropriately
- Getting a mirror out at the table
- Starting to discuss business before the conclusion of the entrée

Be polite to yourself as well. Thank yourself for your networking success—whether for attending an event and meeting some contacts you want to follow up with or landing a new job or a new piece of business as a result of a contact who developed into a trusted advisor or advocate. You deserve it! Watch, realize, and appreciate all the opportunities that have developed due to your new-and-improved networking awareness and good manners.

7

Leading the Way

Networking is a leadership skill. To be a really successful leader, you need to continually hone this skill. Stand up and be a leader by accepting a position on the board of your professional or community organization. Raise your hand and volunteer to work on important projects and organize events, mentor new members or employees, or teach a subject you know well at an organizational workshop or seminar. Arrange public speaking engagements for yourself to present your knowledge of a particular subject and show that you are a leader in your field. If you are shy, try writing and publishing articles in professional or organizational publications to show you are a leader. Create your own website as a marketing tool and as a way to share your knowledge and expertise with others.

Tip 1: Ways to Look Like a Leader

What does a leader look like? You—especially if you have these leadership qualities:

- **Great attitude.** Show you are interested in people and eager to learn more about them. Increase your attractiveness to others by actively listening and showing a sincere interest in what they have to say.

- **Strong belief.** You must have a firm knowledge of and belief in what you are promoting. Believe in yourself and your product or service.

- **Passion.** Do what you love and love what you do. Once others can see that, things start to happen. You put the ball into motion.

- **Ability to reach out and touch someone.** This is where your networking skills really come into play: You've learned how to listen so you know how to help your contact and you don't hesitate to do it.

- **Ability to ask open-ended questions and listen to the answers.** Others know you are truly interested when you ask a question such as "How did you get started in your business/profession?" and you actually listen when they tell their story.

- **Ability to be unique.** What makes you different? This is not only a key to successful networking, it will also be a key to your business success. Be able to articulate first to yourself and then to others about why someone may want to utilize your services rather than your competitor's.

- **Ability to always have a gift.** Give more than you expect to receive. Remember the Law of Reciprocity: No matter how small the gift, they won't forget it. I'm firmly convinced that those who give, receive other gifts in return from others in great abundance.

- **Organizational skills.** Be a true Boy Scout or Girl Scout. Always be ready for every occasion and be organized in your workplace. Always carry a pen and business cards for exchange or to write yourself notes for follow-up contacts.

- **Ability to say "thank you" sincerely.** How many times have you heard "Let's get together" or "I'll call you" and the contact ends there? Take the initiative! Send a note or give a call. Always make it from the heart.

- **Ability to be real.** Most people have their own internal lie detectors and can spot a phony a mile away. Don't activate one—get out of your head and get into your heart!

Tip 2: Ways to Act Like a Leader Wherever You Are

How do you act like a leader? Follow these guidelines:

- **Know that your reputation is valuable.** It often reaches people before you do. Be sincere, honest, prepared, professional, thorough, efficient—and *deliver.*

- **Do what you say you're going to do.** Getting noticed takes hard work, but it's a very small part of the total picture. You must also follow through!

- **Return *all* forms of electronic communication.**

- **Treat everyone with respect and courtesy.** A person's position in life should have absolutely nothing to do with how you interact with them. Remember what goes around comes around.

- **Be visible.** Go to professional seminars, luncheons, receptions, dinners, or any kind of gathering of folks.

- **When you meet people, be mindful.** Look them in the eye, smile, be personable, and have a firm handshake.

- **Develop a knack for remembering names.** You'll be surprised at how positively people react when you remember their name after only a brief introduction. It also helps to take good notes about things you learned from a previous encounter, so you can remember them the next time you meet a contact. Information on family, important dates, and recent key events or projects can all be included in a computer file to jog your memory—and show you're interested.

- **Be an active listener.** This has been discussed a number of times in this book, so you know how important it is.

- **Create a "small talk" notebook.** This book should contain anecdotes and/or questions you've jotted down about life or current events that are guaranteed to stimulate conversation.

- **Be sensitive to the body language** of those with whom you come in contact. Be aware of how you come across to others.

- **Send a follow-up note** to people you've met with whom you'd like to keep in touch.

- **Get to know the support staff** of the person or company with which you want to do business.

- **Know your profession.** Stay abreast of all the latest trends and developments in your field and your geographic area. Read everything you can get your hands on and know who is doing what, where, when, and how.

- **Pass articles along with a note** if you come across one that may be of interest to a co-worker or colleague.

- **Keep a supply of greeting cards** for all occasions.

- **Write, write, *write*.** Send letters to people you want to do business with. Say, "hello," "congratulations," or "I like your work/ your style/your recent remarks about...."

- **Go through your business contact list or database periodically** and send a hello note to those people you want to remember you.

- **Let people know that you are available** to speak or participate in panel discussions, seminars, clubs, religious organizations, civic groups, charitable organizations, service groups, and community centers.

- **Selectively donate your services** to nonprofit organizations that may be in need of your expertise. Give of your time and expertise generously. Be known as the "go-to" person for your particular specialty. Remember to be a resource to others.

- **Remember what Mom used to tell you** and say "thank you." It's amazing how few people invest the time to express gratitude for a favor or a job well done. Remember that people *don't have to do anything* for you. Develop a "thank-you" style that is flexible and works for you; then make this professional courtesy a habit. It will make you stand out in a world where so few people take the time or the trouble to do this.

Tip 3: Be a Leader at Business Functions

How do you recognize leaders at a business function? Here are the qualities that help them stand out:

- They have the ability to make others feel comfortable.

- They appear confident and at ease.

- They have the ability to laugh at themselves—not at others.
- They show interest in others: They maintain eye contact, self-disclose, ask questions, and actively listen.
- They extend themselves to others, leaning into a greeting with a firm handshake and a smile.
- They convey a sense of enthusiasm and energy.
- They are well rounded, well informed, well intentioned, and well mannered.
- They know vignettes or stories of actual events that are interesting, humorous, and appropriate.
- They convey respect and genuinely like people.

Here are some leadership qualities for the office:

- Keep things professional all the time.
- Know the protocol of the firm.
- Listen more than you speak.
- Don't criticize others.
- Help others get what they want.
- Create win/win solutions.
- Be assertive, not aggressive.
- Be willing to go the extra mile.
- Be appreciative of the help you get.
- Work with dedication and loyalty.
- Constantly improve your knowledge.
- Be the best at what you do.
- Learn to get along with everyone.
- Be diplomatic.

Tip 4: Show Networking Leadership in Your Own Office

When the economy is hot, people leave companies without hesitation for more money and/or more prestige. Yet studies still show us that money is not the only motivator that keeps people loyal and productive at their current company.

Here are some great nonmonetary "networking" ways to motivate your team:

- **Say a word of thanks.** Yes, a sincere thank-you from the right person (you) at the right time can mean a lot to a member of your team. Part of the power of this thanks comes because you took the time to note some achievement they've made. Do it in a couple ways—tell the person and write them a card. And here's a special tip: Send the card to their home so that their spouse or family can share in the gratitude. This goes a long way, and it is only human nature that people will respect it.

- **Give praise.** As the saying goes, "praise pays." Tell your staff what they did right and be specific. Know their communication style and deliver the message in the way they understand it. Some people like public praise; others find it is embarrassing. Honor your employee by knowing which one they will accept. Remember to give credit where it's due and consider starting a recognition award in your company. Mary Kay Ash, the founder of Mary Kay Cosmetics, said there are two things people want more than sex and money—and that's praise and recognition!

- **Become a great listener.** Make regular eye contact with employees when they are confiding in you. Ask open-ended questions for clarification. Show concern. Restate or paraphrase back what they've said. Pay close attention and do not let your mind wander. Don't interrupt!

- **Follow through.** If you promise something, deliver. This is how trust and loyalty are built.

Tip 5: "Who Packs Your Parachute?"

Many people only speak to or connect with people they think are important. I'm here to tell you that in order to be a successful networker and leader, everyone must be important.

Consider the story of Charles Plumb, who was a U.S. Navy jet pilot during the Vietnam War. He spent time in a prison because after 75 combat missions, his plane was hit and he was ejected and parachuted to safety—into the arms of the Viet Cong, however.

Some years after he was released, he and his wife were out to dinner one night when a man approached him and said, "You're Plumb, and you flew jet fighters in Vietnam from the aircraft carrier Kitty Hawk. You were shot down!" Plumb looked at him in astonishment and asked how he knew.

"I packed your parachute," the man replied. "I guess it worked!" Plumb gasped both in surprise and gratitude.

That night he could not sleep. He wondered what the parachute-packer had looked like in a Navy uniform. "Did I ever say 'good morning' to him? I hope I didn't ignore him because I was a fighter pilot and he was 'just' a sailor." He thought about how hard this fellow and others like him had worked, making sure that the chute would open. They'd actually held the fate of a flyer they didn't know in their hands. As a public speaker, Plumb began asking his audiences, "Who packs your parachute?"

We all have people who help us get through the day—very often in small, yet major ways. Take the time to keep people in your sights, no matter how busy you are facing the challenges of life. Say "hello," "please," and "thank you," congratulate someone on something that has happened to them, give a compliment, or just do something nice for no reason. This tip packs volumes—just do it!

Tip 6: Organizing and Keeping Track of Your Network

Leaders keep records about all their contacts, so they can respond to them as individuals. Some great new software packages are available that you can customize to your needs, or you can keep index cards if that suits you better. You must develop your own system to keep in touch with everyone in your network on a regular basis. As your list grows, divide it into categories and have a contact plan for each one—quality versus quantity. Make sure you "touch" those closest to you often.

Regularly review your contact list and "clean out" those contacts who, for whatever reason, are no longer in your life. Last summer, I had what I thought was a major setback. While I was overseas, my newsletter was being sent out back home. Somehow someone with the new server we used was a bit careless and hit the wrong button, which resulted in me becoming a "spam queen" within minutes. I was mortified and did not know what to do except send a massive apology. Afterward, I decided to really comb through the list. I had over 5,000 names on it. Some were people to whom others had forwarded the newsletter, so the list had continued growing.

I decided to rebuild my list organically, starting with the people who first wanted to be in touch with me, and to get my newsletter only to those who asked to be on the list. It now stands at 1,100 names, and keeps growing—yet I do know every person now on there.

Make and record notes about each meeting with someone and refer to your notes when communicating. This is easily done on your contact management system and can be linked to your handheld device for easy access when you're on the road. I download this continually from Outlook to my iPhone. I have all my information at hand and updated all the time.

Develop your system for filing business cards, depending on how you plan to use them in the future. Enter them into your contact management system with special notes for follow-up. Take action now. I am a true stickler on this point.

Refer back to Chapter 4, "Building Relationships," for a handy list of all the information I gather for each of my contacts. Into my computer database, I first enter basic contact. In a separate field, I then enter the contact's preferred method of communication: "E" for email, "V" for voicemail, "P" for phone, "T" for text, or "SM" for social media.

Other information I know about them goes in the "Details" section. In the "Activities" section, I enter information such as work-related information, personal interests, what food they like, what books they like, a favorite restaurant, sports activities, and family information, including names of spouse and children.

I add categories, as necessary, that are helpful for sorting, such as the following:

- Category (client, prospect, supplier, professional, or personal)
- "Hot" contact (need to follow up more frequently)
- Source of contact (referral, organization, event, meeting, and so on)
- Ideas and referrals they have given me, including thank-you chain contacts
- Gift history (gifts and premiums sent, the date, and the occasion)
- Holiday cards sent
- Designation (either A, B, or C, which is my method of prioritizing contacts)

Tip 7: Be a Leader for Your Customers: The 7/11 Rule

In the first seven seconds of contact, a customer forms 11 impressions about you and your organization. Is it fair? No, because they are sometimes wrong, but yet we all do it.

Here's what they'll rate you on:

1. Opening impression (friendly, open, and so on)
2. Attractive
3. Credible
4. Knowledgeable
5. Responsive
6. Friendly

7. Empathetic

8. Courteous

9. Confident

10. Professional

11. Helpful

And they make one of three decisions:

1. They dislike you.

2. They are indifferent.

3. They love you.

Now review the leadership qualities we've been discussing, and you'll know how to look like the kind of leader customers trust.

Tip 8: Think Client Retention

Client value is the total benefit (tangible and intangible) that you, your business partners, and your coalition provide to a client throughout the life of the relationship. There's no better way to gain perspective on each and every client relationship, or to predict the impact of every management decision on long-term revenue goals. Here are some tips on increasing client value:

- Identify and document your ideal customer. Get very specific. What are their job functions, key frustrations, buying behavior, lifestyle, age, willingness to advise you on new offerings, and typical spending habits with your firm? Do they value expertise and are they willing to pay a premium for good service, or are they transactional buyers who only care about price (à la Walmart)? Write down the percentage of firms in your portfolio that fit each description.

- Keep a journal for one week detailing how much time you're spending with your ideal customer. The next week, track how much time you are spending with your "less-than-ideal" customer. The third week, list three ways you can streamline the way you work with your less-than-ideal customer, beginning one month from the day you make the list. This may include everything from referring them to another firm to delegating them to a more junior associate, to asking them to pay you in a more efficient way (such as via PayPal.com).

- Guesstimate how much your ideal customer will buy from you during the entire buyer/seller relationship. For example, if you are a consultant, and a typical client stays with you for two years, paying you $10,000 a month, then the current lifetime direct transaction value of a client is $10,000 × 24 months = $240,000.

- Guesstimate how much business each client will refer to you over the next two years. Let's say the typical client sends you one new client every two years at $10,000 a month. That's $240,000 in referral value.

- If you have an advisory team of customers helping you design or launch new products or services, estimate the value of one successful sale for that new offering based on your customers' input.

- Provide your ideal clients with one free service, trial offer, or referral—just to show them how much you value the relationship. No expectations, period. Make this year your season for giving unconditionally.

- Create and regularly administer a low-cost survey to find out how your ideal clients define, receive, and measure value.

- Create a "Master Mind" group of professionals within your organization dedicated exclusively to defining, attracting, and creating lifelong clients and learning from each other.

- Create a referral network of companies, clients, and individuals. Share this with your clients and update it often.

Client retention and development is critical to all we are discussing in this book. This is what a true leader thinks about. One of my favorite quotes is, "A leader is a good manager, yet a manager is not always a good leader." Decide which you are.

Tip 9: The P.O.W.E.R. of Preparation

Be prepared, have your plan of action, stay calm, and ask for what you want. Conduct yourself with authority and P.O.W.E.R.:

P   **"Prepare**, prepare, prepare," said Winston Churchill. Essentially when you make a call, you are making a pitch or a presentation. Prepare in advance what you want to say.

O   Develop an **outline**. Know what you want to say from beginning to end.

W   **Walk** in the customer's shoes. When you speak with your client, hear them out and listen. You will learn something during the process.

E   **Enter** the stage, strongly and confidently. Shakespeare said that we're all actors on this stage called life. If your client is like a lion and your approach is like a lamb, you might be devoured!

R   **Rapport** will build bridges. You've heard the expression, "Love your friends and love your enemies more." Build the relationship.

In any case, the P.O.W.E.R. you have is often in your hands. Take action!

Tip 10: Executive Networking: The Next Step Up

As senior and seasoned professionals, much of our discussion involves topics and tips that you already use and make part of your life.

Moving forward and upward to continue your networking growth, see if the following suggestions can be worked into your lifestyle:

- **Go where other senior execs go.** Attend associate and industry meetings specifically targeted for your executive status. Although general networking meetings at your local industry meeting might be excellent for your staff, your time is better used mixing with other senior people from different companies to help open doors for your frontline people.

- **Pursue high-net-worth hobbies.** Many senior executives meet at the golf club, country club, tennis court, and fundraising art gallery openings. Figure out your interests and then get involved.

- **Volunteer to speak.** Share your industry knowledge, but research the profiles of attendees before offering yourself as a speaker to make sure these are the type of new contacts you need to impress.

- **Do some internal research.** For instance, touch base with your sales and marketing staff to find out what history your company has with some of the business leaders you'll be meeting. This way, if there is something good to bring up, you can use it during your conversation.

- **Prepare your self-marketing message.** Your company is key. However, your personal message can really be a door opener. Think about what part of your personal experiences and background will be of interest to your peers. This might be related to labor relations or how you coped with new government regulations. Show how you creatively handled problems that you know others are facing, and become a resource.

As a senior executive, you are in a unique position to foster, build, and cultivate new relationships. Just remember that networking is a process that, with respect and patience, can create business connections that last a lifetime.

Tip 11: Leadership Techniques at Trade Shows

Realize that all eyes are on you at trade shows, which are like big supermarkets, with people going down the aisles looking for the products that are most appealing. Assuming that all the booths have dynamite fixtures and support materials, then the only thing separating them are the people. Customers start making an impression of you 30 feet from your booth as they're approaching.

Here are some ways to get their attention:

- **Smile.** It disarms almost everybody. Make your smile sincere and warm, and be genuinely happy to see the visitors as they approach your booth. It's a great opener to see a pleasant and enthusiastic face.

- **Stand tall.** We project more confidence and demonstrate that we are interested in meeting people when we stand rather than sit. We've all seen salespeople who are lounging in their chairs and look like the last thing they want to do is get up and greet someone.

- **Don't eat.** Eat only at your breaks; and when you do, make the snack or meal healthy and light. The last thing you want is to appear lethargic at the booth. Also, stock up on bottled water, breath mints, and power bars. Be careful of eating fatty foods that slow you down, and also avoid getting "wired" by drinking too much coffee.

- **Make sure you look marvelous.** Although a trade show is one place that demands dressing professionally, keep comfort in mind as well. Tight-fitting clothing will definitely impact your comfort while selling. And if you're wearing something that has pockets, avoid putting your hands in them—it makes you look unapproachable.

- **Your feet will have an impact on the rest of your body.** Wear comfortable shoes because you'll be on your feet all day. This is also not the time to break in a pair of new shoes. There are too many stories of those who left the show at night practically crippled with blisters and sores from not wearing the right shoes.

- **Wear your badge on your right side.** The reason is that our eyes naturally flow in the same direction as the person's hand we're shaking, which makes it easier for people to see your name tag. Also be careful to shake in a firm and professional manner. If your palms sweat, dry them off periodically so clients don't get a clammy grip.

- **Speak with your guests and not to your fellow "exhibitors."** Make it easy for people to come up to the booth. By nature, people don't like to approach strangers in a group. When you do engage in a conversation with a prospect, listen more than you speak. Remember, in person you have the advantage of watching the other person's body language. Determine if what the other person says matches how they feel about working with you.

- **Perception is reality.** Your booth area is a reflection of you and your company. Keep it clean, neat, and orderly. Be careful not to give away too much literature to everyone who walks by. Instead, be particular, and only give people what they specifically have an interest in. Remember that you can always send information to them after the show.

Studies tell us that most of your collateral material ends up in the wastebasket because the attendees want to carry home as little as possible. They know you'll follow up and send it to them again anyway. Research has shown that you'll have a 50-percent better chance of having your material read if you mail it to them after the show. This also gives you a reason to follow up with a telephone call to find out if they have received the information.

Tip 12: Techniques to Separate You from the Tradeshow Competition

To gain the competitive edge at all the conferences and meetings you attend, incorporate the following ideas and suggestions:

- **The name game.** We all would like to be able to remember names better, especially at a trade show where we're meeting many new people. Practice some of the techniques described in previous chapters, such as keeping eye contact so you remember faces, repeating the person's name when you respond to an introduction, and associating something else with their name.

- **Postcards from the show.** Imagine what it's like being prospective clients at a trade show. When these people come home from the show, they are inundated with salespeople mailing them all their typical follow-up catalogs and brochures. So how can you stand out in this crowd? Send clients a postcard from the city you've just been visiting. Now think of this: Mr. Client returns back to his office several days later, and as he glances through the mail, he sees a postcard from Chicago, from which he has just returned. He turns it over and it says, "Dear Mr. Client: It was great seeing you at the show. Thanks for your time. As suggested, I'll follow up in the next week. All my best." Now, do you think you'll be remembered among all the other people he saw at the show? Yes. I do this daily at the shows. I send out about 25 postcards at the end of each day so that I'm sure the postcards will get to the potential clients in a timely fashion.

- **Give yourself a break.** Trade shows can be stressful and can take their toll on us if we're not careful. Here are a few tips to practice every day:

  - Do some deep-breathing exercises to clear your head.

  - Eat well-balanced meals and avoid excessive amounts of sugar, caffeine, fat, salt, and additives.

  - Get enough rest. Have the discipline to decline a few late-night parties or outings. Remember, if planned correctly, you'll know what meetings are critical and which are less important.

  - Get some exercise. Most hotels have an exercise room. This might even be another alternative selling opportunity. I've met contacts next to me on the Stairmaster.

- **There's no place like home.** Bring part of your home environment with you, such as pictures of loved ones, your own pillow, fresh flowers in your room, or your smartphone with some of your favorite music.

The idea of maximizing your trade show efforts is to have a plan, be organized, pace yourself, and work smart so that you bring home some bottom-line benefits.

Tip 13: Eleven Tips for Success as You Battle Through the Trade Shows

Being prepared and making everything you do look seamless is the key to tradeshow success:

1. Smile. It's the universal greeting.

2. Have fun working. Be patient and inject humor when possible.

3. Keep it simple. Find ways to simplify the selling process.

4. Show character. It takes forever to build relationships, and they can be ruined by one improper action or word.

5. Be kind and nice to everyone you meet at the show.

6. Make your company proud by demonstrating the best customer service.

7. Do what you promised to do after the show.

8. Be economical. Watch your expenses on the road; most things cost more than at home.

9. Be patient. Everyone may not respond positively to you the first time; give people time.

10. Work to improve your selling efforts at the booth. You may need to revise your plan as the show progresses.

11. Be original and unique. Find out what parts of your personality people respond to positively.

Before you finish, here are some questions that can help you better plan the next trade show:

What pre-show planning would you do now that you had not thought of before?

_____

_____

_____

How do you define the purpose of attending a trade show?

_____

_____

_____

What can you plan at an exhibition that will directly improve sales?

_____

_____

_____

How can you upstage the competition?

_____

_____

_____

What has your company done in the past that has succeeded or failed at trade shows?

_____

_____

_____

"Booth camp" is now over. When you follow these techniques, you'll find yourself in better shape to win over customers.

Tip 14: Secret Qualities of Great Business Communications

The mysterious qualities that make one person charismatic and likeable and another less so have been contemplated by philosophers and business people throughout the years. Listed here are the qualities that the finest communicators *always* possess:

- They are confident and are able to ask for what they want.
- They appreciate those that help them.
- They consistently nurture relationships.
- They are tenacious in going around obstacles.
- They are excellent listeners.

- They rebound quickly and completely from rejection.

- They are friendly and approachable.

Don't forget these tips for managing your email correspondence:

- Set aside a specific time (or times) in the day to read and answer email.

- Use the "in-box" method: Make a separate folder for each major individual or group with whom you are working.

- Answer immediately all the email you can.

- Forward those that can be handled by others.

- Save newsletters and other reading material for later in the day.

- Delete the rest.

- Finally, if you have to read a message later, save it as "new."

Tip 15: Motivation for Change

You *can* change your life! For each area of your life (family, career, health, and so on), ask yourself the following questions:

- What do I want to start doing?

- What do I want to stop doing?

- What do I want to keep doing?

- Start making *active choices*. So much of what we do, we do without thinking. Let's say you have set a goal for yourself to have more money in the bank. You are out shopping and suddenly you find yourself preparing to buy something you don't need. Ask yourself: Do I want more money in the bank or do I want this product? Make an active choice based on your own goals.

- Learn to say no. We have been taught to say yes. Saying yes means our lives are often too busy with things we don't want, so there is no room for the things we do want. Saying no means focusing on the things you do want. This one takes practice. Also, always say no in a positive way.

- Find role models. When you really like what someone stands for, what their legacy is, pay attention and find ways to model your life on theirs.

- Focus on what you want, *not* on what you don't want. There is a saying that what you focus on, grows. So, if you are busy focusing on what you don't want to have, you are focusing on the negative. Focus instead on the positive and notice how things change, including the way you feel about things.

- Take it "one step at a time." Making changes in your life is like learning to walk as a baby: You've got to focus on the positive, follow your instincts, and take it one step at a time!

- Leverage it up. Start where you are and work your way up. Take an honest and realistic assessment of where you are now and start from there. Leverage what you have now into something more. Take your current skills and expand them. Find ways to make them grow into what you want them to be.

- Be grateful and *great*-ful. Be full of your own greatness, and be grateful that you have it. Being full of your own greatness doesn't mean having a huge ego! It does mean recognizing and accepting that you are great—at one thing or several things.

- Be prepared. We are so often running around trying to catch up that being prepared seems a dream. Being prepared is the single most important thing you can do to increase your personal effectiveness. Making time to be prepared means slowing down to the pace of life. This will allow you to enjoy the moment, be connected, and be in tune with what is happening around you. It will also demonstrate your leadership.

- Laugh—find humor everywhere. Laughter is an incredible thing. Find ways to laugh every day. Find humor in a situation where you never saw humor before.

Tip 16: Excuses or Blockers to Leadership

Now that you've read about leadership, do you still find yourself excusing yourself from getting on with success by saying any of the following?

- There's not enough money.

- It's too much effort to do... consistently.

- I have a language or cultural barrier.

- I already do too much to do all these other things.

I hear these excuses a lot, and I realize that we all make many choices in life. Some of us have more on our plates than others. This is why I say, "Take the best and leave the rest." Do just one new thing or add one new tip into your life and make it work for you. It can even be an "a-ha moment" in which you say, "I am already doing this. I just didn't know it was networking or relationship marketing." Make just one thing work for you in your life.

You have the chance to learn something valuable today. Whether the day is frenzied or peaceful, stressful or relaxing, there is much you can learn from living in it. Some people let life's lessons slip by unnoticed. Others take them to heart, eagerly and often. Life offers its lessons to all. And life richly rewards those who accept and appreciate them. You could complain that something doesn't work, or you could learn to make it work. You can allow the setbacks to discourage you, or you can let the setbacks teach you how to get ahead.

From every experience, there is a lesson. From every person, from every situation, from every success, and especially from every disappointment, there is something to be learned. Learn all you can from those lessons.

Tip 17: If You Are on Time, You Are Late

Always arrive five to ten minutes early to get settled. I learned this when I was 22 and had my first business breakfast. My mentor, Gil, told me "always get to the location early to be ready to go when your client or guest arrives." I think of this every time I go anywhere. It has served me well.

Tip 18: Golden Circle of Strategic Networking

As I created my Golden Circle of Networking (shown in Figure 7.1), I thought long and hard about the true components of that initial interaction with someone new or someone you are deepening a relationship with. As you connect with someone, make a point to learn something new about them in your discussion. As you are connecting, give something back to them, such as a piece of advice, a suggestion, or something you can send them. Then take away a piece of information you can use later, which can go back to something you learned as you were conversing and connecting. Always thank them for their time and then, if it is someone you had a solid connection with, find a way to follow up with them so that you can continue the conversation and rapport at a later date.

Circe of Strategic Networking

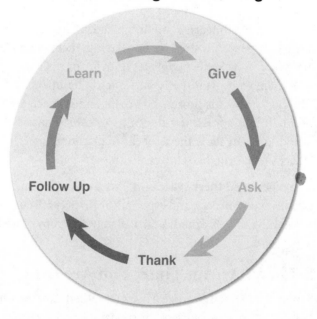

Figure 7.1 Golden Circle of Strategic Networking

A

Six-Month Weekly Networking Reminders

Everything discussed in this book will help you get more out of your professional and personal life when you *apply* what you learn and incorporate the tips into your everyday dealings. So, focus on the positive, and start making *active choices* that will lead to change and take it "one step at a time."

This appendix is designed to help you do just that: The following essential tips are organized into easy-to-follow sections to allow you to practice two a week. Log your experiences as you go along. Feel free to jot down notes on the lines provided. Some of the tips will no doubt come more easily to you than others, so use your observations to help you discover what works best for you.

Following this action plan over time means that within six months, you will have polished your skills, improved your personal networking savvy, and made new, more positive habits. Because even though making changes in how you network and connect with people will take time, commitment, and effort, the benefits can be incalculable.

Week One

1. Give yourself permission to network. Maintaining a positive attitude is the first step toward networking success.

2. Smile when meeting people, entering a room, or talking on the phone. A smile is the first step in building rapport. Smile for 10 seconds when you enter a room.

What I observed this week: what worked, what didn't, and why?

_____

_____

_____

Week Two

3. Make a list of "opening lines" to use when meeting someone new. Use open-ended questions that require more than a one-word answer to create dialogue.

4. Develop a 20-second infomercial about yourself. Practice it until it becomes spontaneous and natural. Create several for different audiences.

Opening lines that worked: _____

_____

_____

My 20-second infomercial: _____

_____

_____

What I observed this week: what worked, what didn't, and why?

_____

_____

_____

Week Three

5. Have a list of "get-to-know-you" questions." These go deeper than "opening line" questions; they help you to get know the interests of the person you have just met. Which ones worked best?

6. Keep a journal of "small talk" topics. These can be about current events, industry topics, books and movies, community topics, and the like.

What I observed this week: what worked, what didn't, and why?

_____

_____

_____

Week Four

7. Do your research before attending an event. Learn the basics about the organization and the people likely to be there.

8. Set a goal for every event or meeting you attend. A good goal is to meet two new people, make a connection, and send a follow-up note, call, or email.

Event and key facts about it: _____

_____

_____

My goals for attending are: _____

_____

_____

Week Five

9. Hone your eye contact: Look everyone in the eye as you speak to them. Doing this shows you are focused on the conversation and interested in what the other person is saying.

10. Focus on your listening skills. Be aware of what the other person is saying instead of thinking about what you will say next. You will remember much more about the person and the conversation.

Notice that the letters in the word *listen* can be rearranged to form the word *silent*: Silence your mind to focus and really listen.

What I observed this week: what worked, what didn't, and why?

_____

_____

_____

Week Six

11. Learn to remember names. This skill will set you apart from most people. Listen carefully when a name is said, repeat it in the conversation, and create a mind picture that will help you associate the person with the name.

12. Give compliments. Make a goal to look for positive attributes and give five compliments a day. Make sure they are sincere.

What I observed this week: what worked, what didn't, and why?

_____

_____

_____

Week Seven

13. Make a list of the key people in your industry or profession who you would like to meet. Determine what organizations, places, and people you know that you could find to help you connect with these key people.

14. Reconnect with four people this week, such as a client or prospect you have not been in touch with for a while, a former business colleague, a former colleague, and a current friend you haven't spoken with for several months.

Key people I'd like to meet: _____

_____

_____

How can I connect with them? _____

_____

_____

This week I have reconnected with: _____

_____

_____

Week Eight

15. Join a networking group, or create one at your office, and go to the meetings. This can be a good place to practice your networking techniques, such as your 20-second infomercial, and keep expanding your circle.

16. Research and join an industry or professional group. Go to two meetings, meet two people, and set up two follow-up meetings before you make your decision to join.

How did the first networking group meeting go? _____

_____

_____

My plans for the next meeting are: _____

_____

_____

The industry group I will join is: _____

_____

_____

What I observed this week: what worked, what didn't, and why?

_____

_____

_____

Week Nine

17. Join a service group, such as a Chamber of Commerce, or a fund-raising organization. Follow your interests in this matter. Join for the sake of giving, not getting.

18. Follow your interest and take a class, join a health club, or take a cruise or special interest vacation. Remember, you need like-minded people in your network.

Which service group will I join and why? _____

_____

_____

How was the first meeting? _____

_____

_____

The special interest activity I will start is: _____

_____

_____

What I observed this week: what worked, what didn't, and why?

_____

_____

_____

Week Ten

19. Volunteer, write an article, or join a committee in your organization. Becoming known helps you meet people and develop relationships faster and more profitably than just attending meetings. Be involved.

20. Send materials or information promised on time or sooner than promised.

How will I become more involved in my organization?

_____

_____

_____

Week Eleven

21. Follow up within 24 hours of a meeting to say, "Nice to meet you" or "Thanks for your time and consideration" and to set another meeting.

22. Call within two weeks of suggesting another meeting. "Let's do lunch" is not an effective networking technique. Make it happen, and set the date.

What was the reaction to the follow up? _____

_____

_____

Date, time, and purpose of next meeting: _____

_____

_____

What I observed this week: what worked, what didn't, and why?

_____

_____

_____

Week Twelve

23. Make sure to thank contacts for referrals and let them know what happened. Keep them in the loop.

24. Send three handwritten notes a day. Send these to people in your network to say "thank you" or "congratulations." Send an article of interest, extend an invitation, or just keep in touch. Use "found time" during the day and make these notes short and simple. Carry notecards and stamps with you. It is your "46-cent investment plan."

Are there any contacts I owe referral status updates to? _____

_____

_____

I will send notes to these people this week: _____

_____

_____

Week Thirteen

25. Write an article or newsletter to send to your contacts. This promotes your business and helps you keep in touch with your contacts and stay on their radar.

26. Become a resource for others. Give generously of your time and expertise.

My article/newsletter topic will be: _____

_____

_____

I could be a resource for: _____

_____

_____

Week Fourteen

27. Send gifts. Remember those who help you, or just remember a special occasion for those in your network. Develop a list of reliable vendors of unique gift items for these occasions. Think of the person and send a gift that was well thought out and picked just for them.

28. Use premiums that constantly remind the recipients of your name and your business. Look for useful items that will be appreciated and that will keep your name in front of others.

To whom in my network would it be appropriate to send a gift and why?

_____

_____

_____

Are there any "signature" gifts or premiums in our organization?

_____

_____

_____

Week Fifteen

29. Look for unique and creative ways to have "face" time with others. Try having coffee or afternoon tea, taking a walk or run, meeting at the sky club between flights, or meeting at an art gallery. Be creative.

30. Remember birthdays and send cards. Find out the birthday month of each of your contacts, make a list of contacts by birthday month, and send out cards once a month to those on the month's list. Also incorporate any special date to remember in this list (this could vary by person).

What creative meetings could I schedule this week and with whom?

_____

_____

_____

Do I know key birthdays and interesting facts? (If not, use this week to start to find them out.)

_____

_____

_____

Week Sixteen

31. Develop a system to keep in touch with everyone in your network on a regular basis. As your list grows, divide it into categories and have a contact plan for each category.

32. Review your list on a regular basis and make sure it is revised and updated.

What system can I use to keep in touch with people? _____

_____

_____

Week Seventeen

33. Develop and maintain a database of your contacts. Your system should work for you; you should not have to work for your system.

34. Collect information about each contact besides the basic contact information. This includes interests, family, awards and promotions, special dates, how you met, and other pertinent facts.

What database system will I use for my contacts? _____

_____

_____

Week Eighteen

35. Determine the way each of your contacts prefers to communicate: phone, email, or in person. Note this on their database record.

36. Make and keep notes about each meeting with each contact. Refer to these when following up or before the next contact with them.

Were there any surprises about what I learned about my contacts?

_____

_____

_____

How will what I learned change the way I relate to them?

_____

_____

_____

Week Nineteen

37. Have a system for filing business cards. As an active networker, you will collect many. Enter the information into your network database and then file the card depending upon how you plan to use it in the future.

38. Enter information about a new contact and follow up within 24 hours of your meeting.

What's the best way for me to store contact information?

_____

_____

_____

Week Twenty

39. Answer your phone and email messages within 24 hours, even when you are on the road. With today's modern technology, you have every reason to be in touch.

40. If you are out of touch for a period, let people know with a message on your phone and an automatic email message. Better yet, check your messages anyway to be the utmost professional.

Week Twenty-One

41. Every day, send an email to someone in your social media address book you have not heard from recently.

42. Once a week, go through your contact list and call three people just to say "hello."

I will send notes to these people this week: _____

_____

_____

What these notes will be about: _____

_____

_____

This week I will reconnect with: _____

_____

_____

Week Twenty-Two

43. Once a month, have lunch with a friend, colleague, or client you have not seen for a while.

44. Send articles and interesting research electronically to keep in touch.

This month I will have lunch with: _____

_____

_____

What happened at the lunch, and are there any next steps? _____

_____

_____

This week I will send articles to: _____

_____

_____

Week Twenty-Three

45. At a company function or meeting, set a goal to sit next to someone new and get to know them. Also plan to follow up with them.

46. If making telephone calls feels uncomfortable to you (or you have a difficult topic to broach with someone), use a script and practice until it comes naturally.

What was the new situation, who did I sit next to, and what are the next steps?

_____

_____

_____

Do I have a challenging phone call to make this week, and how should I prepare for it?

_____

_____

_____

Week Twenty-Four

47. Begin a conversation with a compliment. This is a wonderful way to start when you may not know what to say to break the ice. Again, be sincere. Separately, try to give at least three compliments to people you interact with each day.

48. How has your 20-second infomercial been working? Should it be updated to reflect a new situation or a new experience? Does it provide the right introduction for you?

How has my compliment strategy been working? What are some observations?

_____

_____

_____

How should I modify my 20-second infomercial? How else can I use it?

_____

_____

_____

What else have I observed this week regarding my networking skills?

_____

_____

_____

Week Twenty-Five

49. When the conversation gets off the topic you want to talk about, use a segue such as "That reminds me of..." to get back to your topic.

50. Set a time limit for new interactions. When spending an entire meeting or event with a group of strangers seems daunting, give yourself permission to leave after a specific amount of time (say, one hour).

What I observed this week: what worked, what didn't, and why?

_____

_____

_____

Week Twenty-Six

51. When eye contact is difficult, just remember that "the eyes are the windows of the soul." Practice making good eye contact. Also, notice how many people don't have good eye contact!

52. Give yourself a reward for your networking success during these past six months. Also, on an on-going basis, think of small treats you can give yourself to keep you motivated, whether for attending an event for an hour or retaining a new client as a result of a networking contact. You deserve it!

Your Accountability Questionnaire

- What have I observed during these past six months? What has worked best?

_____

_____

_____

_____

_____

- What didn't work?

_____

_____

_____

_____

- How have my business relationships changed, and how have I evolved as a professional?

_____

_____

_____

_____

- What additional opportunities have developed because of my new skills?

_____

_____

_____

_____

_____

- My reward for completing my networking improvement program will be:

_____

_____

_____

_____

_____

- What ongoing incentives shall I select, if any?

_____

_____

_____

_____

I hope that you benefit from the tools, rules, ideas, and techniques of essential networking. You can incorporate every single thing I have described in this book—from attitude and techniques, to continuity and organization—into your daily life starting now! Remember...

- **Attitude**—Networking is a lifelong process.

- **Techniques**—You have all the techniques at hand to make it happen.

- **People**—Every contact you make is a chance to learn something new.

- **Organization**—Keeping contacts and information at your fingertips is easy and rewarding.

Happy networking and continued success!

Index

F

F.A.C.E., 33-34, 87
face time, 125
face-to-face connections, 33-34
facilitator role, 25
first impressions, 24-25, 30
Five Emotional Time Wasters, 14
follow up, 53-54, 59, 72-73, 123
    act immediately, 13
    notes, 54-55
    Power of Three, 73-74
food, 78
friends, 56
friendship, 7
FYI notes, 81

G

Georgeou, Steven, 59
get-to-know-you questions, 89-90, 118
gifts, 16-17, 53-54, 70, 80, 125
goals, 10, 89, 119
    for events you are attending, 60
Golden Circle of Networking, 115-116
golf network, 7
gratitude, 100
    relationships, 57-58
greetings, 78
groups, joining, 40-41

H

handwritten notes, 53, 61, 124
holiday cards, 53
holidays, 125
humor, 114

I

identifying, potential contacts, 72
image collections, 30
image you project, 24-25
individuality, 25
industry groups, joining, 40-41, 121
infomercials, 56-57, 74-75, 88, 118, 130
information banks, contacts, 45-47
innovation, 17

integrity, 10
interests, following, 41
introducing others, 25
introductions, etiquette, 82-83
introverts, 84-85

J

JetBlue, 19
JoAnn, 37-38
joining
    conversations, 78
    groups, 40-41, 121
    organizations, 66-67
    service groups, 122

K

keeping in touch, 59, 128-129
    developing a system for, 126
    gifts, 70
keeping score, 50
keeping track of your network, 101-103
key people, 120
kindness, 38-39
    Who packs your parachute?, 101
Klein, Don, 39

L

Lamb, Bob, 28
Lambert, Jon, 39
laughter, 114
leadership, 95
    being a leader at business functions,
        98-99
    being a leader to your customers,
        103-104
    executive networking, 106-107
    P.O.W.E.R., 106
    showing networking leadership in
        your office, 100
    at trade shows, 107-109
    ways to act like a leader, 96-98
    ways to look like a leader, 95-96
leadership excuses, 114-115
learning by listening, 35
LinkedIn, 40

listening, 35, 59, 73
  becoming a better listener, 35-36
listening skills, 85-86, 119
long-range questions, 90
lunch dates, 129

M

M.A.G.I.C., 10-11
managing time, 13-14
manners. *See* etiquette
marketing plans, 51
meals, etiquette, 92-93
meet someone new, 129
meet ups, creative ideas for, 87
meeting people, 59
meetings, follow up, 54-55
Michelle, 13
Mother Teresa, 2
motivation, 10-11
  for change, 113-114

N

nail salons, 64
name dropping, 37
name tags, 77
names
  remembering, 36, 120
  trade shows, 109
neighbors, 56
networking
  ABCs of networking, 7-8
  benefits of, example, 67
  DNA (dedicated networking always), 6-7
  as a mindset, 6
  people you know, 8-9
  truth about networking, 68-69
networking action plans, 71
networking domino effect, 40
networking groups, joining, 121
networking leadership, showing in your own office, 100
networking skills, practicing, 65
networks, organizing and keeping track of, 101-103
never assume, 35

new contacts, being prepared for, 70-71
newsletters
  tracking so you can send articles to people, 62
  writing, 124
nice-talking-to-you notes, 82
Nicole, 12
Nierenberg's Rules of Order, 82-83
non-networking events, etiquette, 83-84
notes, 54-55, 80-81
  congratulations, 81-82
  FYI notes, 81
  nice talking to you notes, 82
  thank-you notes, 81

O

opening lines, 88, 118
opportunities for networking, 11-12
  complaints, 48-49
  don't waste opportunities, 34-35
organizational skills, 96
organizations, joining, 40-41, 66-67
organizing your network, 101-103
out of touch, 128

P

Paladino, Jeannette, 28
Palazza, James, 17
passion, 95
pay attention, 60-61
PBS (personal brand statement), 22-23, 74
people
  determining who you would like to meet, 40
  keeping in touch, 128-129
  key people, 120
  meeting, 59
  networking with those you already know, 8-9
  reconnecting with, 40, 69, 120
  remembering those who help you, 17
  showing others you value them, 32-33
  those you want in your network, 49